The Everyday Artefacts of World Politics

This book examines the everyday artefacts of world politics: the things that everyday people make that tell stories about how the world works.

The author argues that people engage in a unique form of multimodal storytelling about the world, their place in the world, and the world they want to live in through the artefacts that they make. Introducing a novel approach to artefact analysis, the book explores textiles, jewellery, and pottery, and urges scholars of global politics to take these artefacts seriously.

Based on original research, this book is inherently interdisciplinary, drawing on concepts and approaches from across the humanities and social sciences, including archaeology, history, sociology, world politics, anthropology, and material studies. It will therefore be of interest to a wide range of readers.

Caitlin Hamilton is a Postdoctoral Research Fellow in Gender, Justice and Security at the University of Sydney, Australia. She is also the Managing Editor of the *Australian Journal of International Affairs*. Previous publications include *Civil Society, Care Labour, and the Women, Peace and Security Agenda* (2021, with Anuradha Mundkur and Laura J. Shepherd), *Understanding Popular Culture and World Politics in the Digital Age* (2016, co-edited with Laura J. Shepherd), and *Popular Culture and World Politics: Theories, Methods, Pedagogies* (2015, co-edited with Federica Caso).

'Developing empirical, theoretical, and methodological innovations, this book is a rare thing: a scholarly work you will actually enjoy reading. Beautifully written and engaging throughout, the book moves us beyond the exceptional and fosters a renewed sense of wonder with which to interrogate the artefacts of world politics, be they ceramics, textiles, jewellery, teaspoons, or something else. This book will be welcome reading for students and scholars of world politics, especially those who have previously been told that what they are interested in isn't really IR'.

Jack Holland, *University of Leeds, UK*

'In this masterful book, Caitlin Hamilton both reminds us that the everyday lives of people are central to global politics and gives us a new way to study these everyday lives through material artefacts. Her methodological work gives the study of International Relations and other fields new tools to think across different levels of analysis and her case studies, from embroidery documenting state atrocities to pieces from the fine art world, push the reader to rethink where and how global politics occur'.

Katie Brennan, *University of Queensland, Australia*

'The everyday is often seen as mundane and of little relevance to the study of International Relations. Not so, argues Caitlin Hamilton, who convincingly demonstrates how a focus on artefacts — textiles, jewellery, and ceramics — can help us see world politics in a new light. In this insightful new book, the stories that make up our political identities come alive and so does the human cost of conflict and violence'.

Roland Bleiker, *University of Queensland, Australia*

'*The Everyday Artefacts of World Politics* boldly confronts the orthodoxy of what we understand to be world politics and encourages us to rethink how we see the world around us. In her effervescent style, Caitlin Hamilton brilliantly examines how the everyday artefacts of our lives have political significance. From embroidered textiles, to the clay that makes our coffee cups, via bracelets made out of bombs, *The Everyday Artefacts of World Politics* is an innovative tour de force that draws together an interdisciplinary menagerie of insights to push the study of popular culture and world politics in an exciting new direction'.

Rhys Crilley, *University of Glasgow, UK*

The Everyday Artefacts of World Politics

Caitlin Hamilton

LONDON AND NEW YORK

First published 2022
by Routledge
2 Park Square, Milton Park, Abingdon, Oxon OX14 4RN

and by Routledge
605 Third Avenue, New York, NY 10158

Routledge is an imprint of the Taylor & Francis Group, an informa business

© 2022 Caitlin Hamilton

The right of Caitlin Hamilton to be identified as author of this work has been asserted in accordance with sections 77 and 78 of the Copyright, Designs and Patents Act 1988.

All rights reserved. No part of this book may be reprinted or reproduced or utilised in any form or by any electronic, mechanical, or other means, now known or hereafter invented, including photocopying and recording, or in any information storage or retrieval system, without permission in writing from the publishers.

Trademark notice: Product or corporate names may be trademarks or registered trademarks, and are used only for identification and explanation without intent to infringe.

British Library Cataloguing-in-Publication Data
A catalogue record for this book is available from the British Library

Library of Congress Cataloging-in-Publication Data
Names: Hamilton, Caitlin, author.
Title: The everyday artefacts of world politics/Caitlin Hamilton.
Description: Abingdon, Oxon; New York, NY: Routledge, 2022. |
Includes bibliographical references and index.
Identifiers: LCCN 2021030888 (print) | LCCN 2021030889 (ebook) |
ISBN 9780367641436 (hardback) | ISBN 9780367641450 (paperback) |
ISBN 9781003122340 (ebook)
Subjects: LCSH: International relations and culture. |
Material culture–Political aspects. | World politics–Social aspects.
Classification: LCC JZ1251 .H36 2022 (print) | LCC JZ1251 (ebook) |
DDC 306.2–dc23
LC record available at https://lccn.loc.gov/2021030888
LC ebook record available at https://lccn.loc.gov/2021030889

ISBN: 978-0-367-64143-6 (hbk)
ISBN: 978-0-367-64145-0 (pbk)
ISBN: 978-1-003-12234-0 (ebk)

DOI: 10.4324/9781003122340

Typeset in Times New Roman
by Deanta Global Publishing Services, Chennai, India

Contents

	List of figures	vii
	Preface	viii
1	**Introducing everyday artefacts of world politics**	1

Everyday 2
Artefacts 6
World politics 8
Everyday artefacts of world politics 10
Notes 12

2	**How to study everyday artefacts of world politics**	14

Notes 21

3	**Textiles**	23

Tapestries of life 25
The wools of war 31
Conclusion 33
Notes 34

4	**Jewellery**	36

From war-worn to worn war 38
Spaces, places, and coal necklaces 42
Conclusion 46
Notes 47

vi *Contents*

5 Ceramics 48

Bringing politics to the (kitchen) table 51
Kneading new stories 56
Conclusion 59
Notes 59

**6 A short reflection on everyday artefacts of world politics
(and all the other questions I still have)** 61

Bibliography 65
Index 85

Figures

3.1	Detail of a Laotian pha pra vet. Source: Author photograph.	28
3.2	Detail of the Keiskamma Tapestry. Source: Reproduced with permission of The Keiskamma Trust.	30
4.1	LOVEbomb plain silver bangle fashioned from recycled aluminium. Source: Author photograph.	37
4.2	Erato Kouloubi, 'Oh no! This is toxic' collection, 2015, *Monomolecular*, neckpiece; tar, bronze, pigment, plastic bag; 50cm × 20cm × 4 cm. Source: Photograph by Alexis Kamitsos. Copyright Erato Koulobi, reproduced with the permission of Erato Koulobi.	45
5.1	Paul Mathieu, *W.T.C. 9-11, 2001, 2002.* Source: Copyright Paul Mathieu, reproduced with the permission of Paul Mathieu.	54
5.2	Penny Byrne, *Sands of Gallipoli (Gallipoli Porn?)* (2015). Repurposed vintage ceramic urn, donated ANZAC Day badges, collected ANZAC Day memorabilia, Rising Sun hat badge, miniature Gallipoli Campaign Service medals, paper collage, emu feathers, ANZAC Day Poppies, custom plinth, PVA, epoxy resin. H × 1900mm W × 700mm D × 330mm. Source: Photograph by Matthew Stanton. Copyright: Penny Byrne, reproduced with the permission of Penny Byrne.	55

Preface

This is not the research that I originally set out to do. I had great ambitions of being a Serious Scholar who studied Serious Scholarly Things – and not just any old Serious Scholarly Things, but the Most Serious of All Serious Scholarly Things: nuclear weapons. I planned to maintain an objective distance from my research, adopt an appropriately scholarly tone, and establish myself as an upstanding member of the discipline of International Relations who demonstrably appreciated the gravity of the subject matter.

But it didn't go to plan. When I first started this research, I was a relative newcomer to the discipline, and somewhat naive to the disciplinary structures and strictures. But what I quickly learned was that looking at the representations of nuclear weapons in pop culture freaked people out. In feedback on one paper, a colleague asked: 'Is this really "relevant" to IR? Or better in anthropology or history?' After a conference presentation, the chair of my panel, a senior professor, pulled me aside after the room had cleared and offered some unsolicited 'paternal advice' that my research into popular culture would be better pursued as a 'side project'. Despite being unfamiliar with the then-growing body of literature in the area, he indicated in no uncertain terms that I would jeopardise my PhD and my future career were I to pursue my line of research. Overwhelmingly, however, the disciplining was much more subtle; when introduced to some prominent academic or other in mainstream IR, they would politely enquire about my research. Usually, a predictable choreography would follow: a slight lean forward of surprise, a word or two by way of platitude, and a swift moving on to another member of the conversational party.

This all left me in a bit of a pickle. I was doing research on nuclear weapons which, although it wasn't really speaking to me, I nonetheless hoped would make me look clever and give me a veneer of professional legitimacy. And it wasn't working. So, there was nothing left to do but to reclaim my research by writing in my own voice and studying the things that mattered to me. What would happen, I wondered, if I started again:

Preface ix

trampled on the boundaries, disregarded them, made my own way through world politics? I began with visits elsewhere – day trips, if you like – to sociology and archaeology and anthropology. I let my attention wander and found world politics in places that I'd never considered before. There was America's then-First Lady Michelle Obama dancing with late-night television host Jimmy Fallon. Nationalism, bipolarity, militarism, heads of states, flags and national anthems were packaged into ten-minute-long vignettes in WWE wrestling matches. I'd switch over to The Food Network and there would be *The Great British Bake Off* offering up stories of homesick American soldiers and morale-boosting 'Doughnut Dollies' in the Second World War. World politics were – are – everywhere and inescapable. And that's how the idea of the everyday artefacts of world politics came about.

None of it would have come into being without Laura Shepherd. I know that a lot of people say that sort of thing and mean it in a really nice way. I'm not sure that I do. It is only because of her sheer persistence, indefatigable prodding, unshakeable faith and low-key but never-ending encouragement – urgh! – that these words became a book. I'm tremendously grateful, obviously, but would prefer it if you didn't tell her that, as it would mean that she was right, and I was wrong and acknowledging that will make continuing to work together nigh impossible. Laura literally read the first word that I wrote for this research and has seen its many growing pains. She is magnificent and I am indescribably lucky and grateful to have her in my life.

Many, many thanks, too, to the fine folk at Routledge – particularly Emily Ross and Hannah Rich, for ushering this project from proposal to publication – and to those at the Gender, Justice and Security Hub. Funding received from UK Research and Innovation through the Global Challenges Research Fund allowed me the time to finish this book, for which I am thankful indeed.

I also owe special thanks to those who gave me permission to reproduce their work: Penny Byrne, Michaela Howse (on behalf of the Keiskamma Trust), Erato Kouloubi, and Paul Mathieu. Their work, and that of the other makers I talk about in the pages that follow, have been such a source of joy and inspiration to me, and without them doing what they do, I couldn't do what I do.

I have also enjoyed the support of a network who have had faith in me and the project, and encouraged me to publish this book, despite my efforts to live my life in peace. They include Nick Apoifis, Nick Bisley, Roland Bleiker, Louise Chappell, Will Clapton, Penny Griffin, Sara Davies, Ian Hall, and Megan MacKenzie. Thank you all for your guidance and support.

Then there's my circle of love, magic, and intuition: Nicole Wegner and Roxani Krystalli. I am in awe of you two. Your support, compassion,

x *Preface*

and wisdom prove a constant source of inspiration to me, and you're the kindest first readers a neurotic writer could ask for. And for my people, who I hold so very dear: Emilie Auton, Guy Dempster, Gabrielle Dunlevy, Lucy Evans, Lucy Hall, Kevin Kwan, Gill Meek, Denise Miles, Jim Milne, Georgia O'Neill, Mia Sheldon, Zahra Stardust, Karen Sum-Ping, Kavitha Suthanthiraraj, and Anna Yanatchkova. My preference is staying in and knitting of an evening, but I would leave the house any time to see each and every one of you. Individually. Not all at once. All at once would make me very anxious indeed.

And, of course, to my wonderful family: Kathryn Bayliss, Margo Bayliss, Mary Bayliss, Richard Bayliss, Jenna, Keith and Milo Hewell, and Andy Kong. Thank you, thank you, thank you.

Finally, my parents: Jane and Keith Hamilton. Dad died in 2007, so wasn't around to see this part of the journey. But my word, how I hope this would have made him proud. And for Mum, who continues to be a source of unconditional love, support, and many shared giggling fits. This is for them.

Caitlin Hamilton
June 2021

1 Introducing everyday artefacts of world politics

This is a book about the everyday artefacts of world politics: the things that ordinary people make which engage in some way with world politics. These kinds of artefacts offer a way of understanding how people see the world, see their place in the world, and live in the world. They are accounts of world politics which reflect lived experience in a way that academic scholarship hasn't always been great at doing.

To get closer to an understanding of world politics that considers everyday lived experience to be important, we need to take everyday artefacts seriously as sources of knowledge about world politics. Doing so also means taking the creation of everyday artefacts as *practices* of world politics. It means being open to finding world politics in places we might not expect, and recognising that world politics involve far more – and far more diverse – actors than much conventional research into the international acknowledges. As such, this book is driven by three questions. What are these everyday artefacts of world politics? How can we study them to learn more about world politics? And if we do study them, what stories can they tell us?

In order to answer these questions, I have made my own artefact of world politics – this book that you are reading. It is driven by a curiosity about how everyday life is implicated in world politics – how everyday people *do* world politics – which, in the words of the great Cynthia Enloe (1993, p. 6), involves 'follow[ing] the breadcrumbs leading from national and international elite decision makers back to the daily lives of people who seem to wield little political influence'.

The breadcrumbs that I'm following are made up of everyday artefacts; the three kinds that I look at in this book are textiles, jewellery, and ceramics: things that people commonly find, use, and make in their everyday. But before I get to them, there are a few concepts that I should briefly introduce: the everyday, artefacts, and world politics. I'll begin by unpacking these deceptively simple ideas one by one and explain how I use them in the rest of the book. Then, after picking apart the concepts,

DOI: 10.4324/9781003122340-1

2 Introducing everyday artefacts

I'll mash them back up into one big concept: that of everyday artefacts of world politics. A brief discussion of how on earth to study these artefacts will follow, before we dive into the really fun stuff – the artefacts themselves.

Everyday

The first part of 'everyday artefacts of world politics' is the everyday. What is it? And where do we find it? Well, the everyday, it turns out, is a bit of a tricky one. It can be 'discouragingly opaque and slippery to study' (Mannergren Selimovic 2019, p. 144). My everyday, and the things in it, probably won't align with your everyday and your everyday things, and neither my everyday nor your everyday will align with everyone else's everydays that are out there in the world. We aren't even safe in the places that seem decidedly *un*everyday, as '[t]here is an everyday in government offices or space stations as well' (Mannergren Selimovic 2019, p. 133). There is, in short, a frustratingly endless multiplicity of everydays, all with their own manifestations of world politics. How, then, can we speak of the 'everyday' as a thing when it means so many very different things?

It might be easier to start with what the everyday *isn't*. The non-everyday: that's the stuff that tends to make the headlines. As Georges Perec, once dubbed the 'most resourceful explorer and indefatigable champion' of the everyday (Sheringham 2006, p. 248), says,

> [r]ailway trains only begin to exist when they are derailed, and the more passengers that are killed, the more the trains exist. Aeroplanes achieve existence only when they are hijacked. The one and only destiny of motor-cars is to drive into plane trees.
>
> (Perec 1997, p. 205)

We are all too familiar with these non-everyday stories; every morning when we open the newspaper, we are faced with 'the spectacle of the distinctly noneveryday; violence, death, catastrophe, the lives of kings and stars' (Lefebvre 1987, p. 11).

These non-everyday events 'shape and shove the everyday' (Björkdahl, Hall and Svensson 2019). People flee their homelands en masse, planes fall from the sky, people are massacred with impunity, and a global pandemic reshapes life as we know it. These are all instances of the 'non-everyday' (or the extraordinary) happening in the space of the everyday, and are the things that International Relations (IR) is well-versed in studying; refugees, terrorism, genocide, and global health are all conventional world politics fare. In fact, as Roger Mac Ginty (2019, p. 237) argues,

Introducing everyday artefacts 3

In many ways, traditional approaches to IR have been a study of the exceptional and outliers. Whether through a focus on exceptional nations, exceptional statesmen (and they usually have been men) (Kisssinger, 1994) or exceptional events, such as war or secession, a key focus has been on order and deviations from it. A steady focus has … been maintained on elites, institutions and borders.

With its 'crises and globalist thinking' (see Acuto 2014, p. 246), IR somewhat prides itself on its focus on the non-everyday; as Robert Keohane (1988, p. 379) noted in his presidential address to the International Studies Association, 'world politics is a matter of wealth and poverty, life and death'. Why bother studying the minutiae when we can instead write about the 'important' people, the big-scale, and the noteworthy?

On top of this, there's a sort of leery distrust around the everyday. As Joe Moran (2007) explains, an unsympathetic assessment of this research agenda is that it involves studying 'the bleeding obvious' (p. 4), because '[w]e expect scholars to have a specialism, a particular expertise that marks them out from non-experts – and when it comes to familiar things like eating prawn sandwiches, crossing the road or sofa-sitting, everyone is a sort of expert' (p. 5). Michael Sheringham similarly identifies the criticism levelled all too often at the study (and the studiers) of the everyday: 'Why linger on what is merely daily? Our duty is to higher things: we are right to shun the ordinary' (2006, p. 22).[1]

But what if, instead of being 'deceivingly trivial and tangible', the everyday is actually 'a complex and fuzzy phenomenon loaded with meaning' (Jacobsen 2009, p. 9; see also Moran 2007, p. 4)? In fact, what if

[t]he smallest details of mundane life can tell us stories about much larger national and global changes. Unconsidered trifles can be clues to more significant, subterranean shifts in society. There is always a reason why we carry out even the most habitual activities – and those reasons are rooted in history, politics and culture.

(Moran 2007, p. 5)

What, then, is International Relations missing by not looking at the everyday? What does the world look like if we look for and listen to these everyday stories?

Where do we begin to find these quotidian, banal, mundane ordinary, vernacular, micro, non-elite, infra-ordinary,[2] everyday things? Georges Perec, theorist of the everyday, implores us to 'question the habitual' and explore 'the banal, the quotidian, the obvious, the common, the ordinary, the infra-ordinary, [and] the background noise' (Perec 1997, p. 206). We

4   *Introducing everyday artefacts*

can look anew at our immediate environment. 'Describe your street', Perec directs his reader. 'Describe another street. Compare. Make an inventory of your pockets, of your bag. Ask yourself about the provenance, the use, what will become of each of the objects you take out'. He concludes with what must be one of the best exhortations of all time: 'Question your teaspoons' (p. 206).[3]

That's all well and good in a kitchen. But what (and, indeed, where) are the teaspoons of world politics? What are the things that have always been present in world politics but never really seen or taken into consideration or written about? How do we move the 'floodlights ... away from the actors who possess proper names and social blazons' (de Certeau 1984, Preface)? The teaspoons of world politics, I think, might be people. Not the presidents and prime ministers, or the heads of global institutions, or the bigwig policymakers – not those people. They're already very visible in world politics. No, what we're looking for is 'ordinary people' (Carver 2010, p. 421); the 'people living normal lives in what are ordinary settings by the standards of their time and place' (Tétreault and Lipschutz 2009, p. 1). They are the people who are

> rarely heard from or seen as actors in world politics, such as the stateless (e.g., displaced persons, illegal migrants, refugees), the illicit (e.g., smugglers, prostitutes, drug traffickers, mafia gangs), and the informalized (e.g., the young, the poor, the illiterate, the feminized, and the 'non-westernised'). These groups affect world politics as much as, and sometimes more so than, their elite counterparts.
>
> (Agathangelou and Ling 2009, p. 67)

Politics lie 'in the midst of the utterly ordinary': 'in the contradictions of lived experience, the most banal and repetitive gestures of everyday life – the commute, the errand, the appointment' (Kaplan and Ross 1987, p. 3). To find these politics, we need to recognise, as Arlene Tickner (2013, p. 214) does, 'that knowledge is rooted in the everyday practices and experiences ... [and] meaningful sense-making activities take place at all levels of society, and are not limited to what is normally defined as "authoritative" within a given field of study'. IR scholars are not the only meaning-makers when it comes to thinking about how the world works. These everyday practices, experiences, and activities that Tickner talks about are a form of theorising – *theory building* – about the ways of the world.

Yet, as a discipline, IR has not paid a great deal attention to everyday theory makers. For too long, the discipline assumed the everyday to be

Introducing everyday artefacts 5

'pre-political, analytically trivial, and causally weightless' (Enloe 2011, p. 447). Even now, as Christine Sylvester (2013a, p. 612) notes,

> [W]hether it is small or large, narrow or expansive, the IR of the moment seems to blink in surprise as key events in the world outpace academic expectations. Is it possible that no matter how reconfigured, much of IR will remain unprepared for the presence, let alone the power, of ordinary people in international relations — people who walk through the Berlin Wall, execute a Velvet Revolution in Central Europe, both events helping shift Cold War polarity, or who toss out autocrats through a series of Middle East revolutions? ... Even as IR gets bigger, broader, and more diverse, the hulking bulk of it relegates people to the sidelines of the international instead of fore-grounding them as key agents of relations of power and change.

That said, feminist IR scholars *have* noted in particular the ways in which conflict permeates the world of everyday actors in all sorts of ways. As Christine Sylvester notes,

> It is not just the 'important' people who affect and are affected by war ... . *Everyday people are involved in the social institution of war in straightforward as well as complicated and often unnoted ways* – as combatants, yes, but also as mourners, protesters, enthusiasts, computer specialists, medical personnel, weapons designers, artists, novelists, journalists, refugees, parents, clergy, child soldiers, and school children.
>
> (2013b, p. 4, emphasis in original)[4]

The everyday has also been theorised as a site of resistance and dissent (see, for example, Crawshaw and Jackson 2011, Kerkvliet 2005, Lilja and Vinthagen 2018, Migdal 2013, and Popovic and Miller 2015); has been an area of focus in peace and conflict studies, particularly with regard to the 'local turn' (see, for example, Autessere 2014, Berents 2018, Mac Ginty 2014, and Sylvester 2013b); and has also gained traction in International Political Economy scholarship (see, for example, Broome 2009, Davies 2016, Elias and Rethel [eds] 2016, Griffin 2015, Hobson and Seabrooke [eds] 2007, and Hoskyns and Rai 2007).

The everyday, then, is a site of study, but it also goes beyond that; as Xavier Guillaume and Jef Huysmans explain, the everyday 'is *more than* a particular kind of site, such as private life, or a particular quality of objects and persons, such as time sheets, everyday political idioms, or military wives, situated at an infra-political level', in that it 'mobilises

6 *Introducing everyday artefacts*

distinct philosophical, sociological and literary lineages that organize our understanding of lives and worlds' (Guillaume and Huysmans 2019, p. 279, emphasis added). It has a sort of normative aspect that rails against a certain way of looking at the world, and at world politics; a way that fails to see people properly. By focusing on '[e]veryday objects, practices and people', we 'bring different conceptions of the international and political life to bear upon scholarly work; conceptions that decentre how politics and political relevance is usually thought through' (Guillaume and Huysmans 2019, p. 281).[5] As Christina Rowley and Jutta Weldes argue (2012, p. 526), we

> need to stop talking about – and very occasionally at (a very small, elite portion of) – the world and start listening to its inhabitants, in order to discover the wealth of what we do not know about how in/securities are theorised and, crucially, how these are theorised in and through everyday practices.

How do we go about listening to the world's 'inhabitants'? Where can we find stories from the everyday? One way to get a sense of what world politics looks like from the everyday, I suggest, is to look at the things that everyday people make.

Artefacts

Artefacts are simply 'things made skilfully', derived from the Latin words for 'thing made' (*fatto*) and 'with skill' (*arte*). Artefacts have an explicitly social dimension; they

> are things that societies and cultures make for their own use … [and can include] photographs, memorabilia, tools, buildings, toys, pottery, jewelry, clothing, weapons, gifts, paintings, graffiti, furniture, and tombstones … written texts such as documents, diaries, journals, memos, meeting minutes, and letters … public records (e.g., birth, marriage, or death certificates), voting records, and newspapers … film, television, and music.
>
> (Norum 2008)

The sheer number of artefacts with which humans engage, and the centrality of artefacts to so much of human activity – 'from a sacred ceremony to the most common craft' (Schiffer 1999, p. 2) – sets us apart from other animals. Vincent Deary sees our artefacts – our things – as so integral to our being that he asks: 'Take all our props away and what are we left with, how are we

Introducing everyday artefacts 7

then?' (2015, p. 68). Taking our things as a focus of study offers an opportunity to 'listen to another voice' (Deetz 1977, p. 161). 'Don't read what we have written', Deetz implores; 'look at what we have done' (1977, p. 161). To this, I might add 'see what we have made'. And boy do we humans like our things:

> Human beings are such incorrigible fidgets, such manipulators of objects, of things we can touch and handle, or think of touching and handling, that it is scarcely possible for us to think, dream and imagine without things exerting their shaping force upon us.
>
> (Connor 2000)

There are a number of near synonyms to 'artefacts', such as 'objects' and things' (Pearce 1994a, p. 9), 'products' and 'goods' (Appadurai 2013), 'commodities' and 'actants' (Woodward 2007, p. 15). What all of these terms have in common, broadly speaking, is that they are used to describe 'selected lumps of the physical world to which cultural value has been ascribed' (Pearce 1994a, p. 9).[6] I personally like the term 'stuff', following the lead of Laura Shepherd (2013b) and Saara Särmä (2014, 2016). Despite seeming as deceptively general as 'thing' or 'object',[7] the choice to use the term 'stuff' in research can be an intentional and meaning-laden choice. As Särmä (2016, p. 186) explains, she 'use[s] the word "stuff", rather than "research material", to emphasise its everydayness and to emphasise that its collection is by no means systematic', and in doing so 'interrupt[s] notions of appropriate and worthy research material' (p. 186).

Studying 'stuff' lets us see the world from a different perspective. Different knowledge – and different ways of knowing – comes from 'each of [our] sensorial domains. A symphony cannot be rendered visually; the aroma of roasting coffee cannot be put into words; the feeling of cashmere or burlap cannot be expressed in music' (Auslander 2005, pp. 1016–1017; see also Howes 2006; Franklin [ed.] 2005; Stiles et al 2011). In a similar vein, it may be the case that words (the primary medium of choice for almost all scholars of world politics) are not the most effective way to express the terror of genocide, the uncertainty of revolution, or the jubilation of liberation.

Mark B. Salter (2015) recognises the importance of things in world politics in his introduction to *Making Things International I: Circuits and Motion*. As he writes (p. vii):

> Things play a crucial role in the assemblage of the international. Borders are made with fences, maps, compasses, passports, guards, and gates. War is made with guns, cell phones, improvised explosive devices, helmets, depleted uranium, aircraft, satellites, electricity, meals ready to

8 *Introducing everyday artefacts*

eat, and oil. Diplomacy is made by telegrams, the Internet, diplomatic pouches, chicken dinners, and cameras. The international economy depends on real and virtual currency, transatlantic cables, weather reports, insurance tables, commodities, ships, and trucks, which in turn depend on pipes, petroleum, steel, and aluminium. Each of these modes of organising international life can exist only when a set of things, actors, and ideas circulate in particular patterns.

From the accoutrements of warfare such as bullets and military vehicles (Saunders 2002), to memorials and architecture – including Saddam Hussein's '"victory arch" … made from a cast of his forearms, showing every bump and follicle' (Rowlands and Tilley 2006, p. 502; see also Sudjic 2011 [2005] on the politics of architecture more broadly) – things matter in world politics. Squares, shrines, statues, palaces, reflection pools, parliament houses and so on; they are all artefacts of world politics (many of which are encountered in the everyday space), acting as a physical manifestation of identities and ideologies.

Even the very concept of artefacts – and the collection thereof – is political through and through; the accumulation of 'curiosities of the world … be it a tool from a distant society, an unusual rock formation, or natural deformity' drove collections across Europe, particularly during the Renaissance (Buchli 2002, p. 4). The material culture of a society was taken as a marker of its social 'progress', and so the study of a society's 'things' purportedly allowed for the measurement of its development (Buchli 2002, p. 2); in the words of Chris Tilley and his co-authors (2006, p. 2), '[t]he West came to know itself and its place in the world primarily through a study of the artefactual Other'.[8]

Things, then – these *artefacts* – matter to world politics in all sorts of ways. We use them to communicate our identities; we document and remember events using them; and they are useful when we want to fight one another and cause a lot of damage. In the concepts of 'everyday' and 'artefacts', then, we now have two pieces of the 'everyday artefacts of world politics' puzzle. We are left with world politics.

World politics

While the last thing I want to do is put anyone off, it would be remiss of me to not warn you that world politics is 'a treacherous domain, since there are multiple incompatible understandings of the field/discipline floating about' (Jackson 2015, pp. 942–943).[9] We can speak of world politics, international affairs, global affairs, global politics, and international politics, and essentially be referring to the same thing. However, many scholars

Introducing everyday artefacts 9

have drawn subtle distinctions, particularly between 'international relations' and the other terms; Mary Ann Tétreault and Ronnie D. Lipschutz (2009, p. 71), for example, note that the difference lies in whether we conceive of world politics narrowly, to capture only the behaviour of states, or more expansively, to incorporate the actions of a broader spectrum of actors:

> 'International relations' refers to how nation-states get along with one another. 'World politics' reflects a more complicated perspective. Nation-states are still in the picture, but so are other corporate actors – firms and banks, labor unions and religious organizations, choral groups and theater companies, sports teams and terrorist cells –and individual persons from the Dixie Chicks to the pope.

Some consider 'international relations' to be the study of states, as well as 'important entities' (Haynes et al. 2011, p. 6) – multinational corporations, international non-governmental organisations, and inter-governmental organisations, for example (Haynes et al. 2011, p. 7). But here, the state still remains the primary unit in this construction of international relations. That's where the idea of the 'global' comes in; Andrew Heywood, for examples, offers a more expansive working definition of 'global' to mean that '[g]lobal politics … takes place not just at a global level, but at and, crucially, across, all levels – worldwide, regional, national, sub-national and so on' (2011 p. 2; see also Mansbach and Taylor 2012, p. 7). This is why, while I'll be using a variety of terms to talk about 'world politics', I won't be using 'international relations' (except to refer to the discipline of International Relations), because of its explicit focus on the state. Instead, I want to make sure that the language I use really centres the 'everyday' (or, at least, doesn't actively decentre it).

What is the 'world' of world politics? Many accounts of the world in which politics take place conceive of the world as in a perpetual state of insecurity, populated by people whose lives are, to borrow Hobbes' fabulously grim and oft-used phrase, 'solitary, poor, nasty, brutish, and short' (Hobbes 1651). But this isn't, thankfully, our only option. We can choose to use approaches that do let us find glimpses of beauty in an altogether more hospitable realm. This can certainly be seen, for example, in L.H.M. Ling's (2014) framing of the world (or, rather, the Multiple Worlds that lie at the heart of her work), which takes into account 'the histories, philosophies, languages, memories, myths, stories, and fables of the human condition' (p. 13) and sees the importance of 'families, while they cook and eat, travel and trade, chat and joke, heal and pray' (p. 14).[10] Unsurprisingly, given the focus of this book, I am very much in the latter camp.

10   *Introducing everyday artefacts*

When you only look at headline-level politics, the world can seem like a relentlessly horrid place, and that is why traditional scholarship doesn't (or, rather, can't) tell us the whole story. By ignoring other narratives about the world, and *from* the world, we only see part of the story of world politics. In order to understand world politics, then – including the beauty and creativity and joy that can be found in world politics alongside the less cheery stuff – we really need to begin by understanding how world politics are lived in the everyday.

Everyday artefacts of world politics

If breaking the idea of 'everyday artefacts of world politics' into its constituent parts didn't sufficiently muddy the waters, squashing it back together into the compound concept sure will. Everyday artefacts of world politics are messy, glorious things.

To start with, not all artefacts are everyday artefacts; a monarch's crown, for example, is not an everyday artefact, though its production process almost certainly has everyday aspects (consider where the jewels were likely sourced, the conditions of their mining, any ongoing dynamics shaped by colonial history, and so on). What counts as an everyday artefact also shifts depending on time and place; artefacts have temporal and spatial aspects. A smartphone was not an everyday artefact in the seventeenth century, nor, in 2015, was it for most of Ethiopia's citizens (Poushter 2016). Conversely, typewriters and VCR players were once everyday artefacts that have now largely fallen out of use (in those particular forms, at least). This is one of the main challenges posed by studying the everyday; as Ágnes Heller rightly notes in *Everyday Life* (1984, p. 54),

> people lead very different everyday lives in a given society, their differentiation turning upon such factors as class, stratum, community, order, etc.; and this in turn means that from the everyday life of any one man, indeed of any one class, we cannot learn everything about the structure of the given society. The everyday life of the serf cannot fully express the structure of feudalism, any more than can the everyday life of the knight.

Then, exhaustingly, comes the question of whether all artefacts are actually artefacts of world politics. Intuitively, I want to say they are. If you drink coffee, own electronic equipment, have wooden furniture, buy flowers, like jewellery, rely on oil, or eat, you are tied to world politics. World politics explain why the laptop I'm typing on was designed in California, assembled in China, and bought in Sydney, and why the water glass from which I'm

Introducing everyday artefacts 11

drinking was produced in Indonesia but bought in Holland. Indeed, having perused my living room while pondering this point, it turns out that I am sharing this very everyday space with a dizzying array of world politics. While there may well be an artefact or two out there that has no world politics story to tell, I find it hard to think what it might be. It's tricky to escape the clutches of world politics; even if you manage to dodge it on one front, you run smack bang into it around the next corner. From the materials used to make something, to the way it's made (who makes it? Where do they make it? Are they paid? Are they paid *fairly*?) and the way it's used or transported or sold or shared or bartered or made into something else ... well, like I said, there's no escaping world politics.

Finally, not all world politics take place in the everyday space, though I do think that all world politics have an everyday aspect; it is hard to think of any major world politics event that didn't have at least echoes or aftershocks (both good and bad) through the everyday. We might not hear about those echoes or aftershocks; when a treaty is signed or a wall comes down (or goes up) or a bomb explodes, these events tend to dominate the headlines – not the people who, as a result, have had to find different ways to earn a living, move around, shop for food, go to school, and so on. I would therefore lean more towards the idea that all world politics can be framed as everyday world politics, and reject the idea that a neat line of division exists between everyday world politics and the world politics made by scholars and policymakers.[11]

Everyday artefacts of world politics highlight the horror and trauma of conflict, and the human cost of war. They also remind us that world politics can be funny and subversive. They can show how people can collaborate for not just bad, but for good as well. And they demonstrate how powerful identity is in the everyday lived experience of world politics. These things deserve our attention and time; as James Deetz (1977, p. 161) puts it,

It is terribly important that the 'small things forgotten' be remembered. For in the seemingly little and insignificant things that accumulate to create a lifetime, the essence of our existence is captured. We must remember these bits and pieces, and we must use them in new and imaginative ways so that a different appreciation for what life is today, and was in the past, can be achieved.

How do we remember – or recognise, or rediscover – these 'small things'? And once we've found them, how do we 'read' them? These are the questions that drive the next chapter.

12 *Introducing everyday artefacts*

Notes

1 I suspect this would have annoyed Henri Lefebvre, philosopher and ardent defender of the everyday, a fair bit. He asks, with suitably outraged incredulity, 'Banality? Why should the study of the banal itself be banal? Are not the surreal, the extraordinary, the surprising, even the magical, also part of the real? Why wouldn't the concept of everydayness reveal the extraordinary in the ordinary?' (1987, p. 9). As he reminds us in his foreword to *Critique of Everyday Life* ([1991] 1958, p. 15) 'the familiar is not necessarily the known'. The everyday, as Lefebvre conceives of it, might even be just a little bit magical: 'On the almost stagnant waters of everyday life there have been mirages, phosphorescent ripples' ([1991] 1958, p. 137).

2 Like infrared light, the ordinary is so ordinary that it often goes unnoticed (Perec 1997, p. 206; see also Moran 2007, p. 3). We only see it, in fact, when it is disturbed by 'the big event, the untoward, the extra-ordinary: the front-page splash, the banner headlines' (Perec 1997, p. 205).

3 Roland Barthes also takes the re-knowing of the familiar as his mode of enquiry, perhaps most famously in the collation of his newspaper columns in *Mythology* (2009 [1957]). In it, Barthes casts his critical eye over a variety of everyday 'myths', including those of wrestling, margarine, and astrology, and everyday artefacts like detergents, toys, and plastic. Aside from being an influential sociological text that established the banal and mundane as valid sites of academic enquiry, this book was also awarded the *L'Express* recommendation for a good holiday read in July 1957 (Badmington in Barthes 2009 [1957], p. ix).

4 Beyond everyday people, everyday spaces can be an attractive target for violence, precisely because of their everydayness – airports, trains, shopping malls, schools and universities, theatres, bars, hotels, and markets; all of these have been targets in recent history because lots of people congregate in these places, which tend to be much less secured (and securable) than the spaces inhabited by the elite actors of world politics.

5 Some other pieces of writing on the everyday that I have found enormously useful in thinking through what I mean when I talk about the everyday include Gardiner (2000); Ginsborg (2005); Guillaume (2011); Highmore (2002); Langley (2008); Lüdke (ed) (1995); Moran (2005); and Smith (1987).

6 While these terms are used somewhat interchangeably, there are subtle differences. The language of 'goods' and 'commodities', for example, are often used by economists, meaning things that have value and can be exchanged (Woodward 2007, p. 15). Taking objects as 'actants', on the other hand, means '[t]hinking about objects as in some ways similar to persons' (Hoskins 2006, p. 78). Jane Bennett draws from this idea, and in *Vibrant Matter* (2009) she explores 'the extent to which human being and thinghood overlap, the extent to which the us and the it slip-slide into each other' (p. 4). In essence, then, taking 'things' as 'actants' means giving them agency (see also Arjun Appadurai's (ed.) *The Social Life of Things* and Mark B. Salter's excellent two-volume edited collection *Making Things International* (2015)). Overly strict demarcation might, however, be somewhat redundant. Indeed, artefacts are often commodities and, depending on one's worldview, may also be actants. Just as theories offer the opportunity to highlight different aspects of the world, so too does the language of things allow us to draw attention to, or downplay, certain aspects of an object.

Introducing everyday artefacts 13

7 Though if one wanted to be pernickety about a distinction between 'thing' and 'object', Ian Woodward (2007, p. 15) offers the following: '"Things" have a concrete and real material existence but the word "things" suggests an inanimate or inert quality, requiring that actors bring things to life through imagination or physical activity. "Objects" are discrete components of material culture that are perceptible by touch or sight.'

8 These collections of things – and places to hold these collections of things, like museums – were central to colonialism, in that they contributed to the processes of 'map making, census inventories and archives as technologies of classification and serialization, which were intended to visibly materialize the totality of a domain over which government power strove to assert mastery' (Shelton 2006, p. 481).

9 This needn't, however, make us too gloomy. We can find solace in Chris Brown and Kirsten Ainley's conclusion that: 'It may simply be the case that International Relations is not the sort of academic discipline where we should expect or welcome consensus and the absence of competing accounts of the world' (2005, p. 11). A few pages later, they write: 'if you want black and white, buy an old television, don't be an IR theorist' (p. 15).

10 So what the world 'is' all depends on how we theorise it. We all have a theory of world politics, whether or not we know it, because 'theory is but the way in which we try to understand the world we live in' (Duvall and Varadarajan 2003, p. 81). Theories aren't optional; everyone has a package of ideas about how the world works. They can be used to diagnose problems or predict how certain actors might behave (Walt 2005, p. 29). They can also 'provide a common vocabulary with which to describe global issues' (p. 35). Theories essentially provide a framework for how to understand, process, and prioritise the infinite pieces of information which the world throws up and which scholars then try to make sense of, and expressions of these understandings of the international take many forms. As such, the same set of facts – or, indeed, the same set of *artefacts* – can give rise to endless different stories (Mansbach and Taylor 2012, p. 9; see also Juneau and Sucharov 2010, p. 173). But the unavoidable problem with theories is that it's simply not possible to tell the whole story; theories mean focusing on some parts of the story, and not on others.

11 Of course, I am not the first to point this out. The body of literature that exists on the Pop Culture World Politics agenda is particularly useful in thinking about the ways in which world politics and culture (including everyday artefacts) overlap. See, for example, Bleiker (2001); Carver (2010); Caso and Hamilton (eds) (2015); Clapton and Shepherd (2016); Grayson, Davies and Philpott (2009); Weldes (2006); and Weldes and Rowley (2015).

2 How to study everyday artefacts of world politics

There are many different ways in which people have studied material culture – or, *things*. Some approaches are especially well suited to particular disciplines; archaeologists, for example, are more likely to get answers to their questions by using methods that help them to date archaeological finds, for example, or ways of excavating sources that don't risk damaging any of the artefacts or structures. But this approach mightn't be of so much use to material engineers, say, who are much more interested in the physical properties of certain materials and how those materials might be put to good use in innovative ways. An art historian, on the hand, might not be so interested in the physical properties of an artwork as they are in what it might tell us about the world in which the painter lived. But knowing that a piece of pottery is 70,000 years old or that a particular kind of fabric might be exceptionally strong, while interesting and important knowledge, doesn't help us to work out what artefacts might say about world politics.[1]

Some of the conceptualisations and methods that we already use in world politics can help us a little bit in how to study the everyday artefacts of world politics – including the idea of actants I briefly noted earlier, along with methods like textual and discourse analysis, and, increasingly, ways of analysing images[2] – but in looking at everyday artefacts, I didn't find these approaches were uncovering the stories I was especially interested in. John Law (2004, p. 2) puts it well:

> Pains and pleasures, hopes and horrors, intuitions and apprehensions, losses and redemptions, mundanities and visions, angels and demons, things that slip and slide, or appear and disappear, change shape or don't have much form at all, unpredictabilities, these are just a few of the phenomena that are hardly caught by social science methods. It may be, of course, that they don't belong to social science at all. But perhaps they do, or partly do, or should do.

DOI: 10.4324/9781003122340-2

How to study everyday artefacts 15

Furthermore, as Jules Prown (1994, p. 133) notes, '[w]e have been taught to retrieve information in abstract form, words, and numbers, but most of us are functionally illiterate when it comes to interpreting information coded in objects'.[3] We aren't taught how to critically 'read' artefacts in the same way that our training equips us to navigate the world of words and, increasingly, images. It's also, quite simply, hard: the 'grammar of things' is 'more complex and difficult to decipher than ... the grammar of words' (Kingery 1996, p. 1). And then the other issue is that artefacts come in so many shapes, uses, sizes, flavours, sounds, and textures, that having any step-by-step prescriptive approach is going to turn into a very general checklist that won't get us any closer to our goal of finding things out about the world politics part of everyday artefacts. So, we need something else.

And that something else, I think, is the idea of storytelling, and specifically multimodal narratives: the idea that we can tell stories using things other than (or as well as) just words or pictures. As I show in this book, we can use textiles, ceramics, and jewellery as ways of telling stories about how the world works, and about who we are. Stories do things, you see – 'they are a primary way by which we make sense of the world around us, produce meanings, articulate intentions, and legitimize actions' (Wibben 2011, p. 2). 'We are born into stories' (Leggo 2008); we are nothing but a set of stories (see Shepherd 2013a). We love stories; '[w]e are, as a species, addicted to story. Even when the body goes to sleep, the mind stays up all night, telling itself stories' (Gottschall 2013, p. xiv).

Stories are powerful – they are full of power: '[h]ow [stories] are told, who tells them, when they're told, how many stories are told, are really dependent on power' (Adichie 2009); they 'have been used to dispossess and to malign ... [also to] empower and to humanize' (Adichie 2009). The process of story*telling* is powerful too: it is 'a fundamentally human way to make sense of the world: to understand its actors, to organize its events, to map causal links between actions and to achieve closure' (Kuusisto 2019, pp. 1–2). We connect through storytelling; we make sense through storytelling. We explain, entertain, and sometimes do harm through storytelling.

World politics scholars are a kind of storyteller; we tell stories about how we think the world works.[4] We tell stories about things that have happened and why we think they have happened. We tell stories about what we think might happen next in the world. We even follow classic storytelling plot structures, as Rikka Kuusisto (2019, p. 1) points out, 'with their respective characters, events and denouements ... tragedies, romances/epics, comedies and ironic/satirical stories'. If we, as IR scholars, are recast as tellers of stories about the world, International Relations becomes 'a place where stories that make sense of our world are spun, where signifying practices about international politics take place, and where meanings about international

16 *How to study everyday artefacts*

life are produced, reproduced, and exchanged' (Weber 2005 [2001], p. 182). This idea of IR as a 'bunch of stories' (Weber 2005 [2001], p. 186) also means that, instead of taking world politics as an ontological fact – a *thing* – we take it as a set of narratives, some of which are more powerful or convincing or repeatedly told than others.

Of course, scholars of world politics are not the only tellers of stories about the world. Storytelling as sense making, information transmitting, community building and world explaining has a long and rich tradition. Although we have claimed the idea of 'narrative analysis' in world politics and other disciplines as an innovative method, and 'storytelling' is a current buzzword in social sciences research, it holds a long-standing and deep importance and cultural resonance for many communities.[5] Most of the stories that IR scholars tell come by way of the written word, though sometimes also through images. There are also oral storytelling traditions, however, and storytelling can be digital, and it can be immersive. Stories can be communicated through art, dance, music, food, videogames, art, film, poetry and beyond (see, for example, Bleiker 2001, 2009; Dittmer 2010, 2013 and 2015; Caso and Hamilton [eds] 2015; Hamilton 2019; Hamilton and Shepherd [eds] 2016; Pruitt 2013; Sylvester 2001, 2009; and Weldes 2003).

If we're open to the idea that world politics is made up of stories, and that stories can come in different forms and be communicated in ways other than (or as well as) words and pictures, then the idea of studying artefacts seems less daunting. We tell stories with words and pictures; but we also tell stories with thread, and with clay, and with precious stones and metals. If world politics are made up of stories, and stories can be told through things, then world politics stories can be (and are) told through everyday artefacts. A piece of embroidered fabric in which someone has stitched tales of political oppression, or a necklace made out of lumps of coal: everyday makers use both artefacts as vehicles to tell their stories. These stories are political, and so too are the artefacts.

As I mentioned above, in IR we have techniques to study political word-stories, and increasingly, ways of studying political picture-stories. The words and pictures are where meaning is made in these stories – we read a book to learn about the aftermath of the atomic bomb dropped on Hiroshima or watch a film (moving pictures) to understand Pol Pot's genocidal regime in Cambodia. Often, stories will be made up of a mix of words and pictures, with one informing the other (graphic novels, like Art Spiegelman's *Maus* (2003), are an excellent example of the magic that can happen between and from the interplay of words and pictures). But sometimes, stories will be made up of more than just words and pictures. The first example that comes to mind is those books for young children that have texture built in. 'Look

How to study everyday artefacts 17

at the sheep!' the text might say, next to a picture of a grinning sheep, with a layer of fluffy fleece. The fleece is neither word nor picture; it's designed to make meaning in a different way for the child: the sense of touch. By feeling the fleece, it is expected that the child will understand something new that words and pictures cannot completely capture – what a sheep feels like. Sometimes, stories might have neither words nor pictures. Beethoven's Symphony No 7, for example, always makes me well up a little (by which I mean, weep). There are no words or pictures involved; this time, it's a case of music – sound – making me feel big feelings.

Stories, then, can be (and often are) *multimodal* in nature; made up of multiple modes of meaning-making. That's just another way of saying that stories often work in more than one way. In the case of the sheep example above, the story is partly told through words, partly told through pictures, and partly told through something else – a sort of fluffy tactility. In the case of Beethoven, the story is told through non-verbal sound. This 'something else' in each case is artefactuality – or what I call 'thinginess'. In the fluff of the sheep's fleece and the soaring crescendo of the orchestra, we understand something that isn't, and maybe can't be, conveyed to us through words or pictures. This might be as straightforward as 'this is sort of what a sheep feels like' or it might be 'behold the depths of human existence that a talented but now dead German composer can make you feel'. Either way, words and pictures – and the ways we've been taught to study these meaning-making things – can't help us to convey precisely the meaning of 'fluffy' or 'inconsolable but nevertheless stoic and hopeful' (in my case, if Beethoven comes on unexpectedly). This means that we need a way to think about, and think through, how to explore and study thinginess.

But actually, all narratives have some sort of thinginess, or artefactual context. Stories always have an artefactual element, whether they come in an illustrated storybook, a colourful cartoon on the television, or performed on stage at the Sydney Opera House. A picture might be published in a newspaper, stuck on a fridge with a magnet, or sent on a postcard, and even if the image itself is the same across all three media, what it means – how we read it – changes depending on its thinginess. A child's school photo has a different meaning if it is framed and placed on a grandparent's mantelpiece compared to if it is printed on the side of milk carton under a label of 'MISSING'. Similarly, different meanings will attach to the same series of words depending on whether they are written on a sticky note and stuck on a computer screen, printed on a street sign, or published in a book. You probably wouldn't take a summons to attend court seriously if you saw me scribble down some words on a paper napkin and hand it to you, but you might (in fact, you probably should) if someone turns up on your doorstep looking serious and holding those same words, but this time written on formal,

18   *How to study everyday artefacts*

court-stamped documents. Even though we generally don't consciously pay a great deal of attention to the thinginess of artefacts, it is always there, and it is important because it's another way of making meaning; artefacts 'have their own form of communicative agency' (Tilley 2002, p. 25). Their thinginess can add to the story.

By throwing artefactuality into the mix, the things we study become unavoidably multimodal. When we start thinking about the thinginess of things, we still have to look at the words and the pictures of the artefact (though not all artefacts will have words or pictures), but on top of that we need to consider all the different ways in which the thinginess might make meaning. Does the artefact make a sound? Is it heavy? Does it smell funny? Where did the bits that became the artefact come from? How (and where) is it displayed? Can you wear it? Is there colour and if so, is it faded?[6] Are there cracks in it? Has it been fixed? Does it drape or is it rigid? Is it soft or coarse? Is it warm or cold? Is it made of natural or manmade materials? Does it taste of something in particular? Is it old or new?[7] Obviously, not all of these questions will be relevant to all artefacts; you probably won't find out much by stroking an internet meme (and please don't go and lick the Magna Carta in the name of research and blame me when you get carted off). Additionally, these questions are by no means exhaustive; you need to meet your artefacts on their own terms. The artefact itself will hopefully give you some clues about where to start – sometimes in the most literal sense: textile enthusiast and rug collector Enrico Mascelloni (2009, p. 25), notes that he has 'spent a lot more time researching in bazaars rather than academic libraries'.

Let me offer a brief example of how artefact analysis might work in practice: arpilleras. Coming out of South American countries including Peru, Chile, and Colombia, arpilleras are essentially fabric pictures (see Adams 2012; Ändra et al 2020; Agosín 1996; McCracken 2011; Snook 2010; Walker 2008). They are often made out of little bits of fabric found around the home and stitched together on a sack that once held flour or potatoes.[8] They are used as a way of telling stories about the lives of their creators; they represent daily activities as well as special events, including

> stories of planting and harvesting potatoes, tomatoes, red peppers, oranges, cabbages, grapes. Stories of spinning, and tending llamas, sheep, cows, horses, and goats. Stories of cousins, neighbors, aunts, uncles, and babies with whom they lived long ago when they were 'at home'.
>
> (Gianturco and Tuttle 2004, p. 68)

How to study everyday artefacts 19

Arpilleras have also been used to make political statements. In Chile in the 1970s and the 1980s, arpilleras became one way in which women could represent the everyday hardships and the crimes committed under Pinochet's military dictatorship (Caldwell 2012). The arpilleras emerging from Peru represented violence even more explicitly. They 'show village massacres, police roundups, and images such as hangings with a background dominated by the unmistakable Andean skyline' (Zeitlin Cooke 2005, p. 21), bearing witness to the atrocities committed by the Chilean and Peruvian authorities.

These fabric stories are particularly powerful, not least because these textiles 'make war seem like infanticide because the figures are so miniaturized, so sweet, so nonthreatening. In fact, it's extremely difficult to convey such extraordinary pain in such a sweet medium' (Kirsehnblatt-Gimblett 2005, p. 51). Despite (or perhaps precisely because of) their unassuming provenance, the arpilleras brought about change. They were smuggled out of both Chile and Peru by various means, including through human rights groups attached to the Catholic Church and by way of diplomatic pouches (The William Benton Museum of Art n.d.; Zeitlin Cooke 2005). This meant that 'these patchwork messages began to travel the world, telling the stories of people whose words could not be spoken or written' (Snook 2010) while simultaneously bringing in income for their creators.

There are three particular artefactual characteristics of arpilleras that I'm going to highlight in order to show how thinginess is a way of making meaning in these stories: colour, the identity of the makers, and the fabrics used. If you look at an arpillera, the first thing you will probably notice is how vividly coloured it is. In some, vibrant blue marks out the skies; in others, little dresses are fashioned out of striking pinks and yellows. Flowers and trees, cacti and baskets of fruits; all jump out from the fabric 'page', both by virtue of their brightness, and thanks to the techniques used which gives the arpilleras depth (some parts of the design are usually padded with a little stuffing, and so literally pop off the surface). These colours belie the very difficult existence that constituted the day-to-day lives of many arpilleristas (makers of arpilleras), and this is one of the characteristics of the pieces that allowed for these artefacts to be sent out of the country: what harm could be done by such bright, happy little pieces of sewn work made by local women?

The assumptions held about the makers of the arpilleras are a second and related thing that adds to the story of arpilleras. Arpilleristas are predominantly female, and preconceptions about the political naivety of women and the innocence of the form that they used to tell their stories meant that arpilleras were subjected to little scrutiny. This allowed female political prisoners to use their arpilleras to smuggle messages out from prison, as

20 *How to study everyday artefacts*

'[e]ven the most suspicious guards did not think to check the appliquéd pictures for messages, since sewing was seen as inconsequential "women's work"' (Gianturco and Tuttle 2004, 67). This is also the reason why arpilleras could be smuggled out of Pinochet's Chile. The artefactuality – the sewn-ness, the fabric, the colours, the figures – meant that documentation of some of the many atrocities committed under his dictatorship were communicated to the outside world, whereas a written or photographic account of the same events would likely have very dangerous if not impossible to create or disseminate (Snook 2010).

A third aspect that can help us understand the 'thinginess' of arpilleras is the fabrics used by arpilleristas. Traditionally, the base canvas of arpilleras consisted of burlap sacks that once held potatoes, flour or grain (Gualberti 2015; Sirch 2015) – fabric that could be found around the houses of women living in even the most pronounced economic hardship. On top of this canvas, arpilleristas use techniques of embroidery and appliqué, incorporating cuttings of their own hair or clothing (Sirch 2015), as well as that of their loved and disappeared ones, including pyjamas and socks (Gualberti 2015). In Peruvian arpilleras, other materials are incorporated into the works; as Ariel Zeitlin Cooke explains, 'the Peruvians fashion little objects from scraps of cloth and attach them to the surface of the cloth, adding bits of wood and imitation leather for the soldiers' machine guns and axes' (2005, p. 21). There are therefore physical traces of the makers and their lives – bits of the things they use and wear, and bits of themselves – literally woven into the pieces; the arpilleristas are part of the work, as are the everyday materials that have featured in their lives, in a material embodiment of their lived experience. This gives the arpilleras a different meaning than if I were to go to my local sewing supplies shop, purchase a variety of materials, and make my own fabric picture even if, on the surface, the arpillera and my efforts were to look similar.

There are many more questions that we could ask of a particular arpillera, but hopefully, this offers some idea of how we can take artefactuality into account when studying an everyday artefact of world politics. Analysing a specific arpillera would mean looking at the 'content' of the particular piece being studied – the words and images – as well as the individual artefactual features of each arpillera and their respective arpillerista. We can use this broad approach to look at other kinds of artefacts. Ultimately, it's a matter of approaching the artefact with curiosity and on its own terms. There are no checklists we can apply; no way of knowing for sure if there are bits of the story that remain untold. And, of course, the story you might find in an artefact will almost always be different from the story I might see in it, and could well be different again from the story the maker of the artefact

How to study everyday artefacts 21

expected us to take away. And that, perhaps, is part of the charm of these artefacts: just like us, these everyday artefacts are filled with complexities and contradictions, joys and sorrows, and the potential for many, many different stories – as we will soon see.

Notes

1 Some scholars working in archaeology and in material culture whose work I have found particularly interesting include Buchli and Lucas 2001; Gaver et al. 1999; Hodder 2003; Gould and Schiffer (eds) (1981); Tilley 1994; and Woodward 2016.

2 Some of the writing that I have found especially useful for textual and discourse analysis include Åhäll and Borg 2013; Cameron 2010; Cameron and Maslen 2010; Der Derian 2005; Doty 1993, 1996; Elshtain 1997; Epstein 2008; Hansen 2006; Lakoff 1991; Lakoff and Johnson 1980; Milliken 1999. And for analysing images, a good place to start is the following: Bleiker 2015; Callahan 2020; Campbell 2007; Cavarero 2000; Dauphinee 2007; Grayson, Davies and Philpott 2009; Kuzma and Haney 2001; Mitchell 1986; Möller 2013; Rose 2001; Rowley 2015 [2010]; Särmä 2012, 2014, 2015, 2016; Shapiro 2009; Wright 2008.

3 Compounding this – or perhaps because of it – artefacts are sometimes seen as 'inferior' despite their significant 'problem-solving potential' (Eighmy 1981, p. 32; see also Brinkman 2012, p. 14, Bristow 2015, p. 47, and Moreland 2001, p. 33).

4 I have found the following (though by no means exhaustive) list of scholarship immensely helpful to think about stories, storytelling, and world politics: Bleiker (1997); Cohn (1987); Dauphinee (2013); Der Derian and Shapiro (eds) (1989); Doty (2010); Edkins (2013); Hagström and Gastafsson (2019) and the other articles in this special issue; Inayatullah (ed.) (2010); Inayatullah and Dauphinee (eds) (2017); Koobak (2014); Mattingly et al. (2002); Minh-ha (1989); the *Journal of Narrative Politics*; Kuusisto (2019); Naumes (2015); Shepherd (2013a) and (2021); Suganami (2008); Wibben (2011); and Weber (2005 [2001]).

5 This includes, for example, yarning, 'an Indigenous cultural form of conversation', which has also been used as a collaborative and relational research method (Bessarab and Ng'andu 2010; see also, for example, Barlo et al 2020; Fredericks et al 2011; Geia et al. 2013; and Walker et al. 2014), Choctaw storytelling (see, for example, Kirwan 2016 and Mould 2003, 2004) and *griot* storytelling of West Africa (see, for example, Ouattara 2018 and, more broadly, Newell 2006). With thanks to Nick Apoifis, who pushed me to reflect on storytelling traditions beyond the academy.

6 See Andersen et al. (2015) on colour in IR. Colour is an interesting one – I oscillate between considering it as something visual and something artefactual. I think I lean towards colour itself counting as a visual thing and then the meaning of the fading, artefactual, but I am very much open to being wrong on this point. Some makers incorporate aspects of their surrounding environment into their work, such as crushed insects or earth for dye (as can be seen in the colcha embroidery that I discuss in Chapter 3) – though this is colour, it's definitely artefactual as well: there's a thinginess to how the colour came to be.

22 *How to study everyday artefacts*

7 Henry Glassie (1999, p. 58 quoted in Olsen 2006, p. 90) offers a lovely, and somewhat poignant, way of how we might read time as an artefactual consideration, taking a Turkish carpet as his example: 'A German couple buy a carpet in the Covered Bazaar in Istanbul. It becomes a souvenir of their trip to Turkey, a reminder of sun on the beach, and it becomes one element in the décor of their home, a part of the assembly that signals their taste. Their son saves it as a family heirloom. To him it means childhood. Germany replaces Turkey. The weaver's memories of village life give way to memories of an aging psychiatrist in Munich for whom the carpet recalls a quiet moment when he lay upon it and marshalled his bright tin troops on a rainy afternoon. Then his son, finding the carpet worn, wads it into a bed for a dog, and his son, finding it tattered in his father's estate, throws it out. It becomes a rag in a landfill, awaiting its archaeologists'.

8 Visit the wonderful Stitched Voices blog at https://stitchedvoices.wordpress.com to see some beautiful examples

3   Textiles

I have Major Alexis Casdagli to thank for first making me see the link between politics and textiles. A member of the British Army fighting in the Second World War, Casdagli was held as a prisoner of war in a Nazi prison camp for four years. He passed the time by sewing; he stitched maps and menus, and sent hand-sewn letters home. He also fashioned more decorative pieces, one of which was displayed by his captors at four different German prison camps. The text, which reads 'This work was done by Major A.T. Casdagli No 3311 while in captivity at Dossel-Warburg Germany. December 1941', is surrounded by a border of alternating hammer-and-sickles, swastikas, and eagles. Rows of stitching lie on both sides of the border, a seemingly random arrangement of dots and dashes added as a decorative flourish. But, of course, the dots and dashes weren't so random; they were actually messages in Morse code. Decoded, the border reads: 'God Save the King' and 'Fuck Hitler'. None the wiser, Casdagli's captors not only exhibited his work, but also tasked him with teaching his fellow prisoners the craft of sewing (see Barkham 2011; Kelly 2011).

This story had particular resonance for me when I came across it while I was doing my PhD, because I was spending a lot of my downtime sewing. Crochet and knitting would come later, but back then, it was all about needle and thread. Christmas cards for the family one year featured little cross-stitched reindeers with beaded red noses. New babies would receive their name stitched under some sort of dinky woodland creature with big eyes; newlyweds a pair of llamas festooned with cheerful bunting. But this was one part of my life, and my research was another. That is, until I came across the tale of Casdagli's subversive needlework, and a whole world of everyday political textiles suddenly opened up for me.[1]

Textiles have occupied, and continue to occupy, multiple complex roles in world politics; according to Elaine Lipson (2012, p. 5), textiles have been 'a form of art, communication, survival, seduction, spirituality, expression, community, and enterprise throughout history' (see also,

DOI: 10.4324/9781003122340-3

24 *Textiles*

on textiles as communication specifically, Andrew 2008; see also Gordon 2013 and Hemmings [ed.] 2015). In some places, '[t]extiles are literally a social fabric which holds communities together via exchange and related obligations' (Florke 2014); in others, they have been used to document heinous war crimes. Competition over the raw materials needed to make textiles was key to Europe's colonial ambitions, and both victories and losses in battle have historically been commemorated on fabric (The Metropolitan Museum of Art 2014). Textiles brought about conflicts between states (Laarhoven 2012), while cotton occupied a central role in the transatlantic slave trade, and textile banners were used in the suffragette movement in the UK (Wheeler 2012), as well as in the Greenham Common protests (Lothian 2014).

Textiles are also used to communicate identity. Tartan in Scotland, for example, is not only used to represent ancestry, but has also been put to work as a symbol of world peace through the design of a World Peace Tartan, which has been worn by the likes of the Dalai Lama, and used to promote nuclear disarmament (World Peace Tartan n.d.). Under legislation passed in 1997, Texas acquired cotton as a state fibre and fabric (Texas State Library and Archives Commission n.d.), while California has its own state tartan (Nieder 2015). Indonesian batik, Indian mirror embroidery, and Zulu woven baskets from South Africa are all hand-crafted artefacts that express cultural identities (Gianturco and Tuttle 2004), as are weavings and embroideries from Mexico, the Andes, Palestine, and Afghanistan (The British Museum 2012), each of which is distinguishable by the choice of technique, material, and colour. Soldiers have made war quilts to document their experiences of war (see, for example, Gero 2015), while Iranian carpetmakers have made rugs that document national politics (see, for example, Schulz 2014). Textile art 'both drives and documents political upheaval' (Westfall 2012).

Today, textiles continue to appear in many areas of global politics, from forced labour in cotton harvests in Uzbekistan (Ramachandra 2020), to communities who embroider their histories and mark rites of passage on textiles (see, for example, Areo and Areo 2012 writing on the Yoruba people of Nigeria); from the cheapened labour of women in garment factories (Enloe 2000 [1989]), to the deforestation created by the demand for forest-based fabrics (see, for example, McCullough 2014); from tourists who are encouraged to visit and buy souvenirs from craft villages, to those living in those same villages whose health and environment often suffers because of toxic chemicals and air pollution resulting from the production processes (see, for example, Dang et al. 2010).

In fact, when you start looking for textiles in world politics, they're absolutely everywhere. Flapping out the front of the United Nations Headquarters in New York. Camouflaging soldiers. Bandaged around the wounds of the injured. Providing shelter, however inadequate, for people living in refugee camps. Being sewn into disposable fast fashion in appalling working conditions in 'sweatshops'. Criss-crossing the planet via well-worn trade routes. Adorning reluctant world leaders attending the annual Asia-Pacific Economic Cooperation (APEC) summit.[2] Textiles have a place in all sorts of world politics stories, from conflicts to colonialism, as well as national identity, human rights, labour conditions, and environmental degradation.

But they also exist in less recognised – but no less political – spaces: kitchens and living rooms, bedrooms and workshops. Everyday people have used textiles to challenge and subvert norms, draw attention to injustices, highlight pressing problems, and celebrate their ethnic or national identities. Textiles have been used as a medium to

> carry the stories of those whom society overlooks: women, children, slaves, immigrants, Aboriginal peoples, housewives, stay-at-home fathers, the ill, the disappeared, the displaced, and the grieving ... Knitting, weaving, embroidery – no matter what the medium is, textiles are both byproducts and generators of narratives.
> (Prain 2014, p. 10; see also Parker 1984)

While we often see pictures of (and read about) the armed forces, flags, and world leaders, far less has been written about the textiles that everyday people make, and the politics of these textiles. And what a shame this is because, as we'll soon see, looking to this everyday space brings to light a rich world of knitted weapons, sewn tales of crimes against humanity, embroidered maps of ethnic identity and nationalism writ large and woolly.

Tapestries of life

When author Deborah Rodriguez visited the annual La Plaza Grande Art and Craft Festival in Mexico City, an embroiderer passed her

> a card that described the embroiderers of her town as story-tellers. We tell our stories with needle and thread. And indeed, when [Rodriguez] looked closely at their work, [she] saw amazingly complex tales of love and marriage, of the harvest, of death.
> (2014, p. 312, emphasis in original)

And she's quite right – textile stories weave some remarkable tales of the ways in which people conceive of their place in the world.

Take, for example, colcha embroidery, which developed in New Mexico under Spanish colonial rule from the seventeenth century onwards (Green

26 *Textiles*

2012, p. 126). Its popularity waned, leaving few skilled colcheras until a revival in the craft in the 1930s (Green 2012, p. 127). Today, it 'remains a vibrant traditional artistic expression anchored in Spanish colonial culture' (p. 127). It is identifiable by the colcha stitch: a long line of wool that is 'tacked down' (Gómez 2011) by shorter stitches which hold the main piece of wool flat against the base fabric, which is traditionally the wool-based *sabanilla*. The stitch was originally used to mend worn bed quilts, by embroidering flowers or religious icons over threadbare sections, but, in the words of Julia Gómez, 'pretty soon, the blanket was covered with beautiful embroidery, and then it became a work of art' (in Gómez 2011).

Colcheras have used colcha embroidery to tell stories on cloth; many pieces of Julia Gómez's colcha work, for example, 'are storied in one way or another ... each one inscribes a story, often interlacing the strands Gómez's life history with the broader account of New Mexico's history' (Erickson 2015, p. 11). Colcheras have, for example, engaged in map-production, using their knowledge of and skills in colcha needlecraft, along with an intimate understanding of a physical place, to make embroidered maps (MacAulay 2000, 2010).

Making colcha needlecraft starts with the materials – shearing coarse-fleeced churro sheep, washing the wool using the sap of the yucca plant, brushing the wool into fibres, fashioning the clean wool into yarn using spindles and spinning wheels (Gómez 2011; see also Nelson 1980), and dyeing using natural colours from insects and native plants:

> [C]hamisa for yellow and onion skin for gold. Madder root turns orange, while green leaches from wild spinach. The cochineal insect, which feasts on prickly pear, produces the rich reds so critical to traditionally embroidered flowers.
>
> (Roberts 2014)

Navajo tea, or cota, is also used for yellow dye, while indigo root is used for blue (Gray 2003).

The finished product is a jumble of material from the colcheras' livestock, earth, and plant sap from flora found in their immediate environment – in the most literal, physical sense – including the insects that had the misfortune to find themselves captured and squashed in the name of art. The land is literally imprinted into these maps; the dyes 'steep native ground into the wool itself' (Erickson 2015, p. 15). The use of these sources of colour are not only meaningful in terms of the aesthetics of the works; they also represent a continuity in the embroiderers' heritage, in that these same pigments were available to the colcheras of years gone by and they continue to be sourced locally (Erickson 2015, p. 15).

Textiles 27

Tiva Trujillo is one particularly well-known colcha embroiderer, whose work includes stitched maps. This is particularly apt because of the already-present associations between the stitching and the land; as Erickson (2015, p. 8) explains, '[t]hrough colcha embroidery, Hispanic identity is deeply anchored to New Mexican territory'. These maps take a fluid approach to space and time, 'conflating past, present and future' (MacAulay 2010, p. 2). In the case of Trujillo's work, the viewer literally gets her perspective of the San Luis Valley; she has flipped the map of the area as it is conventionally represented, 'revers[ing] the usual cartographic arrangement oriented toward north' (MacAulay 2010, p. 2). She represents San Luis Valley explicitly from her viewpoint, replete with miniaturised mountains, roads, grasslands, and waterways. Interestingly, Trujillo places herself not quite at the centre of San Luis Valley, but not far off; in the middle of the bottom third or so of the piece, she has signed and titled her work. Trujillo, and her San Luis Valley, are right there, unambiguously present in the work, surrounded by tractors and lorries, roads and fields, churches and shops, just as she would have been in her everyday life.[3]

Tiva Trujillo and her map-making colchera peers are in good company; the Hmong people of South East Asia create 'pha pra vet', or storytelling cloths (see Figure 3.1 for an example of the pha pra vet which I have hanging on my office wall), some of which also take the form of 'embroidered maps, which engage in complex and nuanced ways with ideas of nation, unity and belonging' (McDougall 2011, p. 62).

These beautiful and narratively intricate cloths recount tales of conflict, forced migration, and folktales, among other things (McDougall 2011, p. 63) including the quotidian activities of life on the land in the case of my pha pra vet. As a result of the Vietnam War and the Laotian Civil War, many Hmong people migrated, predominantly to Thailand.[4] Once in Thai refugee camps, Hmong refugees began to tell their stories of their experiences and journeys through the medium of embroidery. Traditionally used to decorate garments, the traditional needlework style of the Hmong was also used to share embroidered life stories (Lor n.d.), particularly through the form of maps. Ruth McDougall (2011, p. 67, emphasis added) describes one such work – a piece by Ia Veng made in 2008 called *Pha pra vet (Story-telling cloth) with Wat Tham Krabok* – as follows:[5]

> On a brightly coloured cloth, tiny, stitched figures hike over borders and balance on rafts and floats trying desperately to cross the winding curves of the Mekong, the river that has played a significant role in the lives and stories of so many. Elsewhere, fertile gardens and valleys are filled with corn and vegetable crops, which are staples of the Hmong people's diet. The landscape is shadowed by aeroplanes or stormed by soldiers clad in green uniforms ... In this work, as in many pha pra vet, threads

28 *Textiles*

Figure 3.1 Detail of a Laotian pha pra vet. Source: Author photograph.

long used for stitching patterns identifying Hmong groups are used to connect and reconnect communities through time and space, transforming cloths into maps of history. Dynamic, complex and connected to life, these are the types of maps that help us better understand our world.

These map embroideries do more than just identify and reproduce the topography of a place; instead, these maps function as (very beautiful)

Textiles 29

links between identity and territory and culture and memory. Taking colcha embroidery and pha pra vet seriously as sources of world politics, then, can show us how world politics are *lived*, and force us to rethink the places and spaces in which world politics take place.

There's another set of quite different textiles that tell stories of identity: tapestries that hang (or have hung) in parliaments around the world. In the Great Hall of Australia's Parliament House, for example, hangs an embroidered frieze that measures 16 metres across and 65 centimetres high. Presented to Parliament as a commemorative piece of art in 1988 (Australian Women's Archives Project 2013), the embroidery was designed by Kay Lawrence, and includes sewn representations of indigenous artwork and ancient Aboriginal rock carving, and the Australian landscape, flora, and fauna. The tapestry features a cast of characters including a shopkeeper, contractors, and miners. Pieces of writing are also woven into the embroidery; an excerpt from Sam Woolagoodjah's poem, *Balai Dreamtime*, is included, as is as a passage from a letter that Mary Thomas, an early female settler, sent home to England (see Parliament House Embroidery Committee 1988). It tells a story of Australia from white settlement to federation, a temporal framing which, in excluding Australia's First Nations' millennia of connection to the land, has deeply political implications.

Scotland's parliament, too, has exhibited a tapestry that represents a history of Scotland. Dubbed 'The Great Tapestry of Scotland', the project was conceived by author Alexander McCall Smith, historian Alistair Moffat, and artist Andrew Crummy and unveiled at the Scottish Parliament in 2013 (The Scottish Parliament 2013).[6] The metre-squared panels represent key moments in Scottish history such as the emergence of Scotland in 8500 BC, the Black Death in the fourteenth century, and the 1817 founding of newspaper *The Scotsman*, as well as Elvis Presley's visit to Prestwick, the cloning of Dolly the Sheep, and – as a last-minute inclusion – Andy Murray's Wimbledon victory (Ailes 2013). Through the tapestry, the thousands of stitchers of The Great Tapestry of Scotland tell stories – their stories – of their history, their country, and their people.

The Keiskamma Tapestry is a third piece of storytelling embroidery (see Figure 3.2). Initiated in 2000 by Carol Hofmeyr and completed in 2004, the Keiskamma Tapestry was first displayed in the South African Houses of Parliament in Cape Town in 2006 (Schmahmann 2011), though it was neither commissioned by the Parliament, nor made with it in mind (Johnson and Rai 2012). The embroiderers, a group of 100 isiXhosa-speaking women (see also Wedderburn 2019), 'meditat[ed] on the work of professional historians and the colonial archive', drawing on them for inspiration when designing the panels (Johnson and Rai 2012; see also Weddderburn 2019). They then embellished the hessian base fabric of the work with

Figure 3.2 Detail of the Keiskamma Tapestry. Source: Reproduced with permission of The Keiskamma Trust.

beads and buttons and yarn (Schmahmann 2011, pp. 160, 173) to depict events stretching from the first Khoisan people, to the Frontier Wars of the eighteenth and nineteenth centuries, through to apartheid and the democratic elections (Jolly 2014; Schmahmann pp. 163–164). The Keiskamma Tapestry has been cited as the inspiration for others' expressions of histories and identities via embroidery, both within South Africa (see, for example, The Keiskamma Trust n.d., Schmahmann 2011, p. 167) and internationally, such as in the case of the Palestinian History Tapestry Project.

These three tapestries represent a 'non-verbal commentary about people, place, and nationhood' (Jones 2003, p.176, speaking in the context of the Australian embroidery); they script versions of (hi)stories in thread. In doing so, they explicitly draw from the lived experience of the stitchers and their forebears; the Keiskamma Tapestry in South Africa, for example, is narrated from

> the perspective of those who were subjugated and thus reveals how first colonialism, and then apartheid policies, resulted in a violation of the independence and rights of people in the Eastern Cape that was sustained over a period of more than 200 years.
> (Schmahmann 2011, p. 164)

As a result, the project constitutes 'a disruption of elite narratives of South African history' (Johnson and Rai 2012).[7] In the case of the Great Tapestry of Scotland, the everyday makers who contributed panels made their own additions:

Along with the great and good, battles and inventions, they've stitched the stories of nameless generations of ordinary Scots and, as is the way of these things, embroidered a little of their own lives into their work as they ate, lived and slept the tapestry.

(Christie 2013)

The everyday makers who were involved in sewing this Tapestry left threaded traces of their own lives – a tiny, out-of-place iPad here, a family tartan there – and those of their ancestors; the bits of the story of Scotland that mattered to them. And these pieces of needlework more broadly all tell stories – albeit very different stories – of what it means to belong to a place or to be forced out of your homeland; of what it means to live as a subjugated minority, or to grapple with the implications of a violent colonial history; or to simply distil many, many thousands of years of history and culture into a single piece of work.[8] Using everyday voices to narrate national histories is powerful; they are not voices that are heard enough in accounts of world politics but they are so important, and can challenge the worldviews of the creators and the viewers of the artefact alike. Recording these voices and listening to these stories constitutes an important act of recognition: that these lives and experiences are deserving of being documented, of being heard, and of being remembered.

The wools of war

Weapons and wool don't intuitively go together. In fact, in many ways, they are opposites: cold metal compared to fuzzy warmth; colours designed to blend surreptitiously into the background versus a veritable rainbow of yarn; and things designed to threaten, maim, and kill as opposed to things designed to protect, comfort, and bring warmth. Which is why the pink triptych that I'm about to discuss is nothing short of remarkable.

Marianne Jørgensen's pink knitted tank is the first piece in this pink triptych. Installed in 2006 in Copenhagen, Jørgensen led a group of volunteers in blanketing an M24 Chaffee Tank from the Second World War (borrowed from the Danish government) with thousands of pink knitted squares (Wallace 2012). Hundreds of knitters contributed more than 4,000 woollen squares 'as a symbolic act of protest against Denmark's involvement in the Iraq war (along with the United States, the UK, and other European nations)' (Wallace 2012). From a distance, the squares make a striking patchwork quilt, but closer inspection reveals that the variation in the squares extends beyond the shades of pink wool; there are different styles of knitting and different aesthetic approaches, including 'single colored, stripes with bows or hearts, loosely knitted, closely knitted, [and] various

32 *Textiles*

knitted patterns' (Jørgensen 2006). People don't tend to break into smiles when standing next to a tank. But it's hard not to when you see the tank: there's the pink, and the size, the embellished treads on the tank, and the pompom that dangles from the tank's gun … it is, in many ways, entirely absurd. But then, so too are defence expenditures, nuclear weapons, and the ever-increasing militarisation of the everyday.

Some eight years after Jørgensen's tank project, Jaine Rose organised a protest against the global arms trade. Rose also used knitted squares contributed by knitters, and again in pink – 'the most wonderful anti-war colour!' (Rose in Corkhill 2016). Collectively, the contributors created a scarf that measured seven miles long when the squares were stitched together. In an act of 'guerrilla wool-fare' (Tapply 2013), protestors stretched the scarf between Aldermaston and Burghfield, Berkshire, which respectively host an atomic weapons establishment site and a plant that manufactures nuclear weapons. Canadian artist Barb Hunt also puts pink wool to work in her antipersonnel installation. This art project, ongoing since 1998 and inspired by Hunt's attendance at an anti-landmine protest in Paris, consists of to-scale knitted replicas of landmines – more than 100 to date (McElroy 2015) – which she constructs with attention to 'the technical aspects of landmine construction and production' (Black and Burisch 2011, p. 209). The knitted landmines vary in shape, size, and shade, reconstructing 'the astounding variety and proliferation of land mines around the globe' (Art Gallery of Ontario 2001).

All three have a strong common theme: they subvert weaponry, with the tanks and nuclear weapons and landmines that lie at the heart of these works. There are also shared artefactual characteristics across Jørgensen's tank, Rose's scarf, and Hunt's landmines that add meaning to these particular thing-stories. The first, and most obvious, commonality is the pinkness – the tank, scarf, and landmines are all made up of shades of pink. Pink is hard to miss, not least when it comes by way of 4,000 knitted panels draped over a 5.5-metre-long, nearly 3-metres-across, 2.5-metre-high M24 Chaffee Tank, or tracks its way through seven miles of British countryside. It draws attention to the aspects of conflict that we're not supposed to see. Pink undoes the work of the tank's camouflage; it shines a spotlight on nuclear facilities surreptitiously nestled in West Berkshire, a region known for its villages and the beauty of its natural woodland environment; it stands starkly against the white walls of a gallery space, drawing attention to weapons that are catastrophically destructive precisely by virtue of their hiddenness. Pink therefore highlights the concealed, feminises the masculinised spaces and objects, and brings the machinery of conflict out into the open for all to see.

These textile artefacts are also all knitted. Knitting has traditionally been perceived 'as a domestic, feminine pursuit' (Daley 2013; see also

Parker 1984); unimportant women's business with 'granny connotations' (Hermann 2012, p. 1). It represents the height of 'triviality, domesticity, non-seriousness' (Russell in Russell and Barnett 1987), but also nurturing and care; Barb Hunt (n.d.) identifies a 'close association' between the craft and 'caring for the body', and she offers bandages and socks for soldiers that were knitted by hand as examples. She takes knitting 'as a metaphor for recuperation, protection, and healing', and sees knitting as offering the power to '[transform] a destructive object into one that can do no harm' (Hunt n.d.).

Within the pink knittedness of the tank, scarf, and landmines, then, lies a sort of gleeful, joyous subversion. The masculinised weapons that are most commonly associated with the public sphere are subverted by feminised accoutrements from the private sphere. Knitted scarves and blankets, items designed for warmth and comfort, nurturing and caring activities, meet the cold, hard metal of tanks and nuclear weapons – items designed to assert power and cause death and destruction; the masculine and feminine, public and domestic, and the extraordinary and the everyday clash together. The scaling-up of the artefacts (in size, for the tank blanket and scarf, and in number for the landmines) functions in a similar way: unlike the tank and military facilities, which intimidate in their occupation of large amounts of space, there is something almost parodic about the scarf and tank-coat writ large. Scarves aren't supposed to stretch for seven miles; blankets and coats aren't designed to fit army tanks; landmines aren't meant to be seen at all. But when they do, we can't help but look, and marvel at the incongruence – the sense of things not being quite where they should be – which, in turn, might make us question what we (think we) know: about conflict, about security, and about world politics.

Conclusion

Textiles are incredibly powerful everyday artefacts of world politics. They are soft and squishy, and bring warmth and comfort. They are overwhelmingly found in private, domestic, everyday and local spaces, like homes and markets. But just when we think we know where to expect them, there they pop up, fashioned into landmines in a museum; as sprawling tales of history and life and politics hanging on the walls of parliament houses; and in a public square, draped over a tank. From thread and fabric cleverly combined come stories of anger, fear, frustration, and disbelief: of weapons that cause devastating injuries, of indigenous and ethnic identities and traditions – some lost, and some carried on – and of oppressed and suppressed histories. At the same time, these textiles tell stories of quiet and joyful resistance. They tell stories of people who are still here, making the

34 *Textiles*

same things in the same way their grandparents and great-grandparents might have made them. They tell stories of survival, and of celebration. These artefacts go to the very heart of who we are, as people who do world politics, and as people who tell stories about how the world works.

Notes

1 'Textiles' is a catch-all term for a number of different ways of making; knitters and crocheters use knitting needles and crochet hooks to make interlocking loops out of yarn, while embroiderers use a needle and thread or yarn to darn or embellish fabric, and might do this by hand or using a sewing machine. Appliqué is a sort of textile collage which involves sticking bits of fabric to another piece of fabric with stitches; quilters use a similar technique to make bits of fabric into a quilt. Then weavers use a loom with a warp and a weft to interlace yarn or strips of fabric to make rugs and mats amongst other things.

2 In some years, leaders have been compelled to wear the host country's national dress for a 'family photo'. Buzzfeed has helpfully compiled their 'definitive ranking' of said outfits (Brown 2017), including the Malaysian batik shirts of the 1998 meeting held in Kuala Lumpur; ponchos in Chile and Peru in 2004 and 2008 respectively; and the Driza-bone jackets of the Sydney-based summit in 2007. My personal favourite? The stunning Ao Dai worn in Hanoi, Vietnam in 2006. Clothing has also been used by other state leaders and public figures to communicate political ideas, such as Mahatma Gandhi's strategic wearing of Indian, hand-woven cotton – 'he learned to use it to communicate his most important messages to followers and opponents and to manipulate social events' (Bean 2015, p. 235) – and the sweater that Bolivian President Evo Morales sported in 2006, made of alpaca wool and featuring a 'native Bolivian design... in keeping with [his] Aymara heritage and his largely populist message' (Bryan-Wilson 2015, p. 288). Clothing has similarly been put to work by everyday people, such as in the case of Palestinian women who, during the Intifada, wore dresses that incorporated the flag of Palestine (Sherwell 1996).

3 See also the work of Josephine Lobato, including *Las Misiones* (1993), for further examples of colcha cartography (MacAuley 2010).

4 In recent years, Thailand has faced criticism for forcibly returning – euphemistically referred to as a 'repatriating' by Thai government officials – thousands of Hmong asylum-seekers back to Laos (see, for example, Mydans 2009 and Médecins Sans Frontières 2008). Once there, reports suggest they face 'conditions [that are] unbearable' (Pao Change quoted in George 2010).

5 This piece measures 150cm by 238cm, and no reproduction that I could include here would do it justice. It is painstaking and colourful and massive and detailed and magnificent, and every time I come across it, I find myself exploring the dozens of stories that are rendered in thread on cloth. A reproduction of the whole work can be found in McDougall (2011, pp. 70–71).

6 That these tapestries hang (or have hung) in houses of parliament around the world matters. Houses of parliament are themselves 'artefacts of political culture' (Goodsell 1988, p. 287); their designs have embedded within them 'complicated questions about power and identity' (Vale 2014, p. 3). As Nelson Goodman (1985) argues, buildings do not just exist, but they also 'mean'; in his words 'we may read of buildings that allude, express, evoke, invoke, comment,

Textiles   35

quote; that are syntactical, literal, metaphorical, dialectical; that are ambiguous or even contradictory!' (p. 644). Parliament houses are the site of 'ceremony and ritual' (Rai 2010), of 'democratic performance' (Parkinson 2012) and, with somewhat surprising frequency, of fistfights (parliamentfights n.d.). They are intrinsically sites of 'high politics', and as such, 'placing an artwork in the seat of government inevitably gives it a political dimension' (Jones 2003).

7 In the case of the Australian Parliament House embroidery, members of the state- and territory-based Embroiderers' Guilds around the country volunteered their time and embroidery skills to the project, with 504 women contributing 12,000 hours of unpaid stitching (Australian Women's Archives Projects 2013). For them, the project was an (exceptionally time-consuming and labour-intensive) hobby. In contrast, the Keiskamma Tapestry was supported by The Keiskamma Trust, a body that is designed to 'foster hope and offer support for the most vulnerable... [and] address the challenges of widespread poverty and disease' (see http://www.ngopulse.org/node/32630). The Keiskamma Tapestry project provided work and training for 100 women from the region. Different again, the Scottish embroidery was created by more than 1,000 people scattered around the country; some were members of embroidery clubs, while others sewed their designated panels in pairs or small groups (The Great Tapestry of Scotland n.d.).

8 This distillation process was not an easy task, as one might expect. Historian Alastair Moffat, who was one of the leaders of the Great Tapestry of Scotland, acknowledged that creating the textile narrative required a 'glorious process of ruthless editing' (in Ailes 2013). He continued: 'Pitfalls open on every side. One of the deepest is the military option, our history as a series of invasions, wars and battles, many of them grey defeats. Most important have been our efforts to make a tapestry that distils Scotland's unique sense of herself, to tell a story only of this place, and without bombast, pomp or ceremony, to ask the heart-swelling rhetorical question: Wha's like us?'. In asking 'Wha's like us?', Moffat references a famous Scottish toast: 'Here's tae us; wha's like us? Gey few, and they're a' deid' – meaning 'here's to us; what's like us? Damn few, and they're all dead'. Although the toast is sometimes erroneously attributed to Robert Burns (see, for example, Macwhirter 2007), Knowles (1999, p. 778) suggests that it probably originated in the nineteenth century, also noting that 'the first line appears in T.W.H. Crosland *The Unspeakable Scot* (1902), and various versions of the second line are current'.

4   Jewellery

As I write these words, I am wearing around my wrist a piece of bomb that was dropped in Laos. During the Vietnam War, the United States dropped some 260 million bombs on Laos across 580,344 bombing missions (BBC 2016). Most of these bombs were anti-personnel cluster bombs, around a third of which did not detonate – meaning that masses of unexploded ordnance were left behind over vast swathes of Laos. Painstaking mine-clearing efforts continue today. But what does one do with do with a dismantled bomb (let alone 75 million of them)? Why, you make jewellery, of course – which is precisely what Sue Mason, the founder of LOVEbomb Jewellery, does in collaboration with artisans from Laos' Xieng Khuang Province. The collection, which includes earrings, necklaces, and simple, silver bangles like mine, is made from recycled bomb aluminium. My bangle is beautiful – a sort of matte, hammered silver (see Figure 4.1). It is also very light but sturdy – there's no give to it – and it retains a surprising amount of body heat after it has been worn for a little while. *And it used to be part of a bomb that was dropped out of a plane.* Its former life is a bit hard to wrap my head around, if I'm to be honest, and I find myself sometimes just staring at it.

Apart from being quite the conversation starter, this bangle is perhaps the most literal artefact of world politics that features in this book. No one is going to argue that bombs aren't world politics, even if they are now jewellery. The creative transformation from bomb into bangle, as we'll soon see through other jewellery artefacts, is also a powerful way of simultaneously remembering and resisting: my bangle prompts (the continuation of) conversations about US aggression in South East Asia, the results of which are still being felt today in many places. It forces us to rethink temporalities of conflict; how echoes of war still rumble through Laos (along with every other country that continues to have to clear mines and dismantle bombs). And it is also thoroughly subversive in the literal sense, subverting war into beauty and weapon into fair income.

DOI: 10.4324/9781003122340-4

Figure 4.1 LOVEbomb plain silver bangle fashioned from recycled aluminium.
Source: Author photograph.

Just like textiles and ceramics, jewellery has a long and political history. From 'seeds, berries and shells', to 'pendants made from the bones and teeth of animals', '[t]he wearing of jewelry has been a constant feature in mankind's existence from earliest times' (Phillips 1996, p. 7). It has been used to mark status, such as a monarch's crown or wedding bands of the married. '[L]ike it or not, jewelry is tightly bound to luxury, excess, and money, which by their very nature underpin political agendas ... It can imply anguish, integrity, or change even as it evokes power' (Cohn 2014). As Aja Raden notes in her wonderfully titled book, *Stoned* (2016), '[p]ieces of jewelry have spawned cultural movements, launched political dynasties, and even started wars, or at least, been major contributing causes of political and military conflict' (p. xi).

There are all sorts of intersections between jewellery and politics. Dog tags, featuring the name, rank, company, and regiment of a soldier, are one kind of adornment that has clear political resonance, used as a form of identification for members of the military on deployment, and as a questionable fashion accessory by others. The Dutch used Venetian glass beads to buy Manhattan, or so the story goes, while the theft of a diamond necklace involving a falsely accused Marie Antoinette contributed to the start of the French Revolution. There are also less grand – but, I should stress, no less political – stories to be told about jewellery; of tiny weapons to be worn around necks, bracelets that represent one of the worst genocides the world

38   *Jewellery*

has ever seen, and rings that speak of environmental destruction, as we'll soon see. But after all is said and done, of my three artefacts, jewellery is perhaps the one that needs its stories the most, because,

> [g]emstones are, in fact, just colorful gravel. They're just rocks that we've given special names. True jewels are things that are beautiful and scarce. We want them because few others can possess them. We want them even more if they are from some very faraway, exotic place. Their value is, and always has been, 90 percent imaginary.
>
> (Raden 2016, p. 6)

Without our stories, diamonds are really nothing more than lumps of carbon that, when they've been cut just right, catch the light in a pretty way.

Jewellery also continues to be a source of intense political wrangling – take the Koh-i Noor, for example. One of the largest cut diamonds that exists, and currently held by the Queen of England, ownership of the Koh-i Noor remains disputed (see Anna Malecka 2018, p. 84). Though it is a centrepiece in Britain's Crown Jewels – it sits in the crown of the Queen consort, last worn by the Queen Mother and placed on her coffin in 2002 (Anand 2016) – the governments of India, Iran, and Pakistan, and the Taliban of Afghanistan, have all made claims on the gem, efforts which the British government have vociferously rebuffed (Boissoneault 2017). And, of course, the Koh-i Noor isn't the only diamond to feature in politics (see Weldes and Rowley 2015). Diamond mines are known for their dire labour conditions and the environmental degradation that results from the pits. They are used by state and non-state actors as a source of finance in the case of 'blood diamonds', or 'conflict diamonds', which are illegally traded with profits used to foment control and fuel conflict (see, for example, Campbell 2002).

Everyday jewellery makers also tap into the deeply political nature of their medium, crafting some remarkable stories. Some make comment on the toll of war on bodies; others critique decisions made by politicians far away from the battlefield. Others still have used jewellery to tell stories of place: of migration, of home, and of the ways that humans are destroying the natural environment. Engaging with these thing-stories gives us the chance to learn more about our world, and the countless ways in which world politics take place.

From war-worn to worn war

Something funny happens when we take weapons out of the context of the military. Instead of the taken-for-granted place that weaponry occupies in

Jewellery 39

conflict, rendering arms in other forms makes us look at them again – or really, perhaps, see them properly for the first time. Small squashy grenades made out of pink yarn heighten how horrifically destructive the real thing is, as we saw in Chapter 3. And it's the same with jewellery; making weapons small and wearable, worn close to the skin, hanging daintily around a neck or a wrist, makes us see weapons anew – just like my bomb bangle did for me. Nancy Meli Walker's necklace *War and Peace Choke Her* also offers a powerful critique of war, driven home in its tininess. In Walker's own words (in Fenn 2017, p. 283):

> The work is a collection of symbols: Chain maille necklace – war through history. Pure white bullet pearls – the innocent life lost in war. Plastic toy guns – exposing our children at an early age to war as if it was a game. A 22k gold peace sign – the preciousness and high value of peace. Blood red teardrop garnets – loss of life/blood and tears cried from war. Chasing and repoussé medieval shields – we should shield ourselves from confrontation and war.

The piece itself doesn't feature text, but its title certainly tallies with this feminist reading of the necklace: it is a close-fitting necklace, or a choker, but the name of the piece, *War and Peace Choke Her*, alludes to the particular price that women tend to pay in conflict – a theme that is well established in feminist IR (see, for example, Cohn [ed.] 2013, Enloe 2000 [1989] and Tickner 2001).

Visually, the necklace is arresting: Walker has arranged the little guns, pearl bullets, and hammered shields with a pleasing symmetry, and a gold peace sign is prominently displayed in the middle. The three garnet teardrops are attached to the chain at the back, so if the necklace were to be fastened, they would hang down the back of the wearer's neck, like drops of blood. The 'base material', so to speak – the chain maille – no longer holds the heaviness that we might associate with the garb of a knight, and instead takes on an airier, more elegant and almost woven texture. The textual and visual aspects therefore tell a story; but it is the artefactual elements of Walker's piece that really drive home the message. It is no coincidence that the things that are precious in a traditional sense – the pearls, the gold, the garnets – are used to represent the same things that scholars of feminist world politics stress when it comes to conflict: the loss of lives, for example, the absolute, incontrovertible necessity of peace, and the emotions of conflict. What value is there in weapons? Here, the guns are throwaway plastic toys, though given the exceedingly slow decomposition of plastic as a material, maybe the symbolism works on multiple levels: weapons, like plastic, are worthless but nigh-impossible to get rid of once and for all.

40   *Jewellery*

Melissa Cameron's RPG series offers another interesting series of jewellery pieces that offers a different way in which artefactuality can tell a story. Her *Ruchnoy Protivotankovy Granatomyot Works* series is made up of a pin of a rocket-propelled grenade launcher (hence the 'RPG' in the title), a pin of an anti-personnel round, and a pendant that takes the rough shape of a garden hand-trowel. While the grenade launcher pin is quite clear in what it is representing through its form, the others are a little more subtle. Their meaning, as Cameron explains (in Fenn 2017, p. 51), lies in their *scale*:

> The chosen scale [1:9] echoes the nine million of these weapons that have been made so far, and the nine countries that still currently manufacture the weapon. The necklace that unfurls from the former hand-trowel is in a strip 2.444 metres in length, or 22 metres at the reduced scale, representative of the over 22 meter lethal radius of this weapon. The smallest pin takes the form of an anti-personnel round, cut into four pieces to show the minimum rate of fire, and is also scaled at 1:9.

The pieces are therefore replete with meaning that isn't textual and isn't really visual either; driving home meaning through the scale of an object is an inherently *artefactual* meaning-making process. The size of something, and the meaning inherent to the size of something, extends beyond the visual, and demonstrates why taking a thing's thinginess into account in our analysis matters. That the neckpiece started off as, and continues roughly to occupy the shape of, a hand-trowel – a quintessentially everyday garden object – only enhances this artefactuality, and the destruction wrought by these weapons.

My third maker here, Stephen F. Saracino, is a metalsmith. Saracino's work is intensely political, and many of his pieces represent his efforts 'to come to grips with the absurdity of a world hell-bent on resolving its problems via violence' (Saracino 1984). *Green Line Sedan*, for example, represents 'the invisible demarcation between East and West Beirut separating Christian and Muslim populations' (Saracino 1993), while *Lockerbie Flight Bracelet* (1995) remembers the 1988 bombing of passenger airline Pan Am Flight 103 over Lockerbie in Scotland. He has also made a war trophy in the form of a bold braceletesque piece.[1] *War Trophy. Nation Building. 3rd Place*, made of sterling silver, is made up of an extended armoured vehicle, featuring a gun and ammunition on the roof of the car and a tangle of soldiers atop the structure, all of which rests upon a solid plinth. Of the piece, Saracino says (in Fenn 2017, p. 234):

> I thought it was well past time to design, fabricate, and distribute trophies for wars, in this case specifically for the category of Nation

Jewellery 41

Building. This trophy is awarded to the United States for its 'efforts' regarding nation building after its ill-conceived, ongoing, and disastrous war in Iraq.

War trophies, of course, have a long history. As Joan E. Cashin (2011, p. 339) explains, talking about the Civil War in the United States,

> The war generated a massive traffic in objects, and it transformed the material culture of the entire country, prompting the redistribution of millions of objects ... Soldiers and civilians ... used the words 'trophy', 'relic', 'souvenir', and 'artifact' interchangeably to describe objects taken during the War. Their behavior reveals a timeless fascination with objects, which convey a multitude of cultural messages that are not always easy to say with words.

What sets Saracino's work apart from the conventional war trophy and gives his commentary a biting edge is that his trophy is not celebrating or fondly remembering anything; *War Trophy. Nation Building. 3rd Place* is the jewellery equivalent of a disdainful slow clap. The United States messed up so badly – criminally so – and in so many different ways, in its 'nation building' project in Iraq that it deserves – nay, demands – recognition. We are not to forget this, Saracino tells us through this piece.

A similar message comes through the work of Bernhard Schobinger, a Swiss artist jeweller with 'a reputation for rebellious innovation' (Manchester Art Gallery 2014). Over the course of his 40-year career, Schobinger has made many pieces, but the one that particularly resonates in the context of the present discussion is *Holiday in Cambodia* (1990), a cuff made out of hammered silver. Outlines of bones and skulls have been hammered into the metal, 'a broad band of whitish silver that is reminiscent of bone' (Den Besten 2011, p. 56). The skulls 'are neither Gothic Revival facsimiles nor religious relics; these skulls are deformed abstractions with sunken eye cavities exhibiting a broken brittleness from being buried in earth for a long time' (Cohn 2014). Needless to say, this is a confronting piece of jewellery. As is the case with Nancy Meli Walker's necklace, which I discussed above,

> [I]t is in that moment of recognition, when the title is linked to the jewelry object, that Schobinger makes his powerful critique. This is no souvenir reflection; it is a cry against inhumanity.

(Cohn 2014)

All four of these pieces – Nancy Meli Walker's *War and Peace Choke Her*, Melissa Cameron's RPG series, Stephen F. Saracino's *War Trophy. Nation*

42 *Jewellery*

Building. *3rd Place* and Bernhard Schobinger's *Holiday in Cambodia* – compel us to remember the cost of war: the blood, the destruction, the catastrophic mistakes, and the murders. They are souvenirs in the most literal, etymological sense: they are collective memory pieces. But there is nothing to celebrate in these memories of war, and of genocide; these aren't memorials of valour, of tales of military bravery. No: these pieces remember brutality and genocide; the very depths of inhumanity, and the horrors that humans wreak upon one another. And they compel us to do the same.

Spaces, places, and coal necklaces

As well as making us think more carefully about what conflict really means, jewellery is used to explore the ideas of spaces and place; both in a physical, architectural sense, but also in our relationship(s) with (a) space – in migration, in belonging, and in exclusion. The work of Australian jewellery artist Su san Cohn is a particularly powerful example of how jewellery can be used to explore ideas of place, and our relationship to places. Two powerful projects that she has produced revolve around the idea of displacement: *Styx* and *Meaning(less)ness*.

Styx, exhibited as part of Cohn's *Uncommon Moments* show in 2015, is made up of a display of nine 8GB USB sticks, made up of ebony, Huon pine, pink gold, and fine silver. As Dylan Rainforth (2105) describes them, '[t]he "welcome" sticks are beautiful but useful: each contains a USB with geographical and cultural information'. The sticks, which can be worn as pendants, are designed to carry vital local information that might be useful to a newly arrived migrant, like 'transport, rubbish days, what the hours of banks are … even the football teams' (Cohn in Ayres 2019). In this sense, they really are 'jewellery as survival kit' (Webb 2015). It is an act of welcoming strangers: 'Styx is jewellery to say welcome, to invite a person without a homeland to enter a new home … [T]he Styx is a magical stick, a message stick with which to negotiate the way into a new community' (Cohn 2015).

Meaning(less)ness, 'a performance combining spoken word, video and jewellery to explore the meaning of objects' (Fairs 2018), came about in response to a law that was enacted in Denmark in 2016. It was known as the 'jewellery law', and it permitted Danish authorities to confiscate assets of over 10,000 kroner from migrants and asylum seekers upon their arrival (Barrett 2019). Wedding and engagement rings were exempted in guidelines, but other valuable possessions – including 'meaningless jewellery' – were fair game (Edgar 2019). Unsurprisingly, the law proved controversial, with some going so far as to draw comparisons with the Holocaust. It

Jewellery 43

also prompted Cohn to visit Copenhagen. This is where she discovered that '[t]he Danish border guards had refused to enforce the legislation … They felt they couldn't judge what was "meaningful" jewellery and what was "meaningless" jewellery' (Cohn in Edgar 2019). Cohn has a theory as to why this is; as she explains,

> The wearer is the person that puts the value and meaning into jewellery by storing their own stories. And those stories are political … People pass something on, or give something, and that becomes a part of someone's history. And I think the politics lies within that.
>
> (Cohn in Clement 2019)

And then there's the material itself that can represent place – the stuff that the artefact is made up of that tells a story. In the case of the three makers I talk about shortly – Kyoko Hashimoto, Erato Kouloubi, and Sophie Carnell – one possible story concerns the many different ways in which we are destroying the environment. Hashimoto, Kouloubi, and Carnell use physical evidence of this – physical pieces of the world – to tell their stories: from coal to concrete, and plastic to tar. Using these raw materials is meaningful in a literal sense – it is the artefactuality of these pieces of jewellery that makes meaning. You could represent coal, for example, using other kinds of materials, but the depth and nuance of meaning in the following artefacts comes directly from their *thinginess*. In this reading of the artefacts, meaning isn't really communicated visually, nor is there a visible textual message; it instead lives in the thinginess of, in this case, coal, tar, and a plastic bag.

Much of Kyoko Hashimoto's work speaks to the degradation of the environment as a result of plastic, concrete, and fossil fuels. Her piece *Coal Necklace*, for example, might prompt us to rethink ideas about value and preciousness. In this necklace, 18 silver settings hold orbs of coal, just as jewellery claws would normally fix a precious stone securely in place. Coal isn't a material that tends to be celebrated in a conventional sense – after all, we burn it, and we threaten to put it in the Christmas stockings of naughty children. It's dirty, and it's an awful polluter. Given the wide availability of other stones that are pretty colours, that glitter and glisten in the light (and that don't leave unsightly smudges on one's decolletage), coal is a funny material to pick. It is also surprisingly difficult to get one's hands on, but worth the hassle; as Hashimoto herself explains (Hashimoto n.d.):

> I have been working with this material for the past 18 months. It charges me with emotion. From the challenge of obtaining it through to the challenge of working it, my relationship with coal has been one

44 *Jewellery*

of respect and reverence. Unable to buy it through normal channels, I forced myself to trespass and take it from decommissioned mines. In the studio, I found coal to have an unparalleled blackness, unlike any other material I've worked. It is lightweight, but dense. It needs diamond tools to carve. It has a beautiful structural irregularity that present as grooves filled with shiny, crystal-like grains. Coal inspires me to imagine the forces of the earth, the geological compression, the massive power and time it took to create, buried within the ground.

In Hashimoto's account, coal has all the attributes that we might usually think of when it comes to gemstones: vivid in colour, lightweight, shiny, unique. There is also, of course, a pleasing irony that in the case of *Coal Necklace*, it is diamond which is being used to fashion the coal into something wearable. The making process of this necklace offered its maker an opportunity to reflect on where the materials came from; the backstory of the coal. In the way that Hashimoto describes it, coal is elevated from something humdrum and unvalued to something really quite magnificent. Through her work, she offers up a different story about coal. The conditions needed to create coal – the old forests of many years gone by, the lack of certain bacteria, the many thousands of years, the physical pressure exerted upon it – makes it quite incredible, which in turn makes the way we use it all the more insulting. Instead of the reverence that Hashimoto brings to coal, it is mined from the earth and burnt, in turn damaging the earth in all sorts of ways. She makes a similar point in the three pieces that make up her 2018 work, *Ritual Objects for the Time of Fossil Capital* (co-produced with Guy Keulemans), which is made out of plastic, concrete, sand, resin, and synthetic rope. The name of another of Hashimoto's series sums up her broad approach perfectly: *Better Worn than Burnt*. We have choices as to how we engage with the world. And currently, Hashimoto's work says, we are very much making the wrong choices.

Erato Kouloubi also uses natural materials – in her case, tar – in order to comment on the damage that we are doing to the environment (see http://eratojewellery.com/collections/). Her use of tar is no accident; she explains that it is commonly founds on the beaches of Greece, where she is from, and she uses it as a material very intentionally 'in order to convey the threat, the fear and the crude death of all living beings that live in nature and are condemned by the humanity'. For example, she created *Bird of Paradise* (2015), a glossy black, tar-coated lightbulb dusted with bronze,

in order to convey the beauty and the ugliness. The tradition, the sounds of the sea, the sand on our beaches in contradiction with the death of all the beings that live under the water and suffer from the ecological disaster.

Also in 2015, she created the five-piece series *Oh no! This is toxic*, made up of a brooch (*Asphyxia*, 2015), two sculptural bracelets (*Chocolate mousse*, 2015, and *What earth taught me*, 2015), a necklace (*Monomolecular*, 2015 – see Figure 4.2), a set of rings (*Tools*, 2015), and a headpiece (*Two bodies cannot occupy the same place*, 2015). As she explains, the work is designed to address environmental issues:

> Human activities are contaminating the world's water systems and disrupting the lives of animals. From toxic chemical runoff to the accumulation of litter, miles away from land. We alter the planet rapidly and we experience the consequences.

Although there are variations across the collection (some are dusted with pigment, while others have pink wool attached, for example), the pieces are united by one key feature: the intimation of thick, sludgy, suffocating oily

Figure 4.2 Erato Kouloubi, 'Oh no! This is toxic' collection, 2015, *Monomolecular*, neckpiece; tar, bronze, pigment, plastic bag; 50cm × 20cm × 4 cm. Source: Photograph by Alexis Kamitsos. Copyright Erato Koulobi, reproduced with the permission of Erato Koulobi.

46   *Jewellery*

tar. It is suspended, mid-drip from the end of the neckpiece, and coagulates into unseemly lumps and bumps around the headpiece; it oozes over the tubes that sit atop the ring and seeps over a brooch. While the shininess of the set tar does admittedly give the pieces a pleasing sheen, its cloying and sticky nature comes through uncomfortably – and almost obscenely – clearly.

Sustainability is at the heart of the work of a third jewellery artist, Australian Sophie Carnell (see https://www.sophiecarnell.com/), who uses found objects to comment on the health of our planet. Her work explores ideas about consumption and waste, as well as value, place, and memory.[2] Using everything from repurposed milk bottles to fishing line that Carnell and her co-makers found and hand dyed for *Sustainable Bling* (2018), and linen tea towels (*I Carry the Moon in a Silver Bag* 2018), Carnell's work draws from – indeed, is *made* from – found objects; things that people either overlook or actively discard. One thing commonly (and mindlessly) discarded is plastic, and it is the material at the heart of *Vanishing Point I, II & III* (2015, 2017 and 2019). The first of the series, *Vanishing Point I*, saw Carnell 'walking along coastlines and collecting bags of big bright ocean debris … and thinking about their effect on fish and sea mammals'. The second and third instalments have focused more closely on micro plastics – tiny particles of plastic that, though small enough to be largely unseeable, do an enormous amount of damage – 'not just on marine life; not just by working their way up the food chain to humans and causing massive health issues; but also by endangering the oceans themselves'.

All of the pieces are made primarily from plastic in its various forms – *Morphing*, for example, is five pairs of brooches created out of plastic knives and forks, ping pong balls, straws, cotton bud sticks, and coral, and *The Ocean is Bleeding* includes disposable contact lenses. Many of these pieces incorporate more traditional stones with the repurposed plastic; the three brooches that are part of Carnell's Urban Coral series, for example, feature recycled peridot alongside plastic spoons and lollipop sticks, while a neckpiece in the same series includes spinel from Tasmania, but mainly started life as a shopping trolley seat recovered during one of Carnell's beachcombing expeditions. Just like Hashimoto and Kouloubi, then, Carnell's work uses – repurposes, rethinks, reconceives of – precisely the *stuff* that she is criticising. And in doing so, she underscores the value of plastic – and the immense costs of the way that we (mis)use it.

Conclusion

I opened this chapter with my Laotian bomb bangle, which represents an act of radical reframing: from bomb to bangle, and weapon to something wearable. The pieces of jewellery that I've looked at in this chapter do something similar, turning weapons into necklaces, making brooches out of fossil fuel, and transforming genocide into jewellery. They are thoroughly, utterly subversive – and thoroughly, utterly political. These makers have made things that are usually burnt into things that are worn; things that are usually ignored into things that cannot be unseen; and things that have been mindlessly discarded into something that is valuable and cherished. They take things and places with a story that we think we know and show that there's an entirely different story (actually, often many entirely different stories) to be told. They also show how powerfully, unapologetically political everyday artefacts can be, from a dusty lump of carbon to a brilliantly gleaming diamond.

Notes

1 I say 'braceletesque' as, while there is, in theory, space for a hand to fit through this piece, the size, shape, design, and weight would make it quite an unwieldy – though certainly statement-making – accessory to throw on with a blazer and a pair of jeans.

2 You may remember me sharing Georges Perec's prompt, 'Question your teaspoons' (1997, p. 206), with you, earlier in this book. Sophie Carnell, incidentally, does just this in her series *Spoons & Ware*. As she says: 'To me spoons, by their very form, are a symbol of giving and generosity, and also of containment. They are a universally recognisable object and one that, in varying degrees of beauty and design, is probably used by everybody everywhere around the world everyday. I love to make spoons that can be both unusual though practical and also ones that question their practicality altogether; to embellish the form of the spoon, to ascribe meaning by changing the form or material of the handle. I just love spoons' (see https://www.sophiecarnell.com/spoons-ware-1) (Carnell). I am inclined to agree, and am also gratified to find that the teaspoons of world politics... might actually literally be teaspoons.

5 Ceramics

While some forms of ceramics are carefully preserved and highly valued (Ming vases come to mind), most are found in more everyday places: in kitchens, in the forms of plates, bowls, teapots, and mugs, perhaps a vase or two in a living room, and maybe a spare mug (if your house is anything like mine) used to store pens on a desk or toothbrushes in the bathroom. There are a mish-mash of different phases of life in these ceramics: there are perhaps three or four plates that have survived from the first set that my parents bought when they first moved in together some 40 years ago; there's my mug from a holiday in Kyoto, glazed in turquoise with a charming duck waddling across an unglazed circle; a mug – gifted from a Vietnamese university after a work collaboration – that is now home to makeup brushes; and a Wedgewood vase (bought on sale) that felt like a pleasingly grown-up purchase in my early twenties. There are also the two wonky glazed bowls that I made last year during a largely unsuccessful short course in wheel pottery, but the less said about that the better.

Ceramics are made of clay.[1] Clay is a natural mineral, the result of rocks decomposing into mineral deposits, often including a variety of impurities (Hamilton 1974, p. 21). Kaolin, or porcelain clay, for example, tends to be made up of silica, alumina, titanium oxide, iron oxide, lime, magnesia, potash, and soda (Hyman 1953, p. 7), with the specific proportions of each mineral changing depending on where it is mined. There are significant deposits of kaolin in China, Czechoslovakia, England, France, and Germany, along with some in Florida, Georgia, and South Carolina in the United States (Tipton 1990, p. 2),[2] all of which vary slightly in composition.[3] But at the end of the day, clay really is no more than 'a variety of mud' (Rawson 1971, p. 12).

The kind of ceramic that you end up with depends on the kind of clay that you start off with and the temperature at which you fire it. Primary clay, such as the kaolin that forms the basis of porcelain, is dug up from where it was formed; in other words, where the rocks originally decomposed

DOI: 10.4324/9781003122340-5

Ceramics 49

(Rawson 1971, p. 24). However, water also often carries clay, leaving sedimentary deposits that might be 'found on the sites of former rivers, lakebeds, estuaries or seas', and mixed up with stones and whatnot (Hamilton, 1974, p. 22). This is the case in secondary clays – such as the clay used to make earthenware, as well as ball clay – which might move multiple times (sometimes over the course of thousands of years), carried along by these various water sources, and its travels change its composition, including by adding new minerals or impurities (Hamilton 1974, pp. 22–23). In any case, deposits of clay are mined or dug out, a process which can have serious environmental consequences including deforestation (see, for example, Sonter et al. 2017) and degradation of waterways (Asante-Kyei and Adddae 2016).

Natural clay needs to be mixed with certain minerals in order to create a 'body' – a material that can be used to make ceramics. There are specific 'recipes' available; the one that Josiah Spode used for the original English Bone China, for example, was 52% bone ash, 24% Cornish stone, and 24% China clay (Tipton 1990, p. 16). Most potters, however, will buy commercially prepared clay, sensibly sparing themselves from measuring out little piles of powdered bone or talc. Then, different kinds of clay-mixtures need to be fired at different temperatures, and end up having different levels of porousness, which results in different effects, which, in turn, makes them suitable for different kinds of things; 'what, for example, is appropriate for a porous unglazed water jug is utterly unsuitable for an acid jar' (Leach 2011, p. 19). Add to that the different modelling, building, throwing, turning, cutting, sealing, glazing, and firing techniques, aesthetic preferences, decorative flourishes, uses, and making processes, and we find ourselves with rich cultural ceramic traditions (see Cooper 2000; Rawson 1971, p. 28).

There is something almost magical about it, really: 'Inert clay, from the earth, is made into something which is directly and intimately related to active craft, to the processes of human survival, and to social and spiritual factors in the life of man, all at once' (Rawson 1971, p. 6). Pottery, as James M. Skibo (1994, p. 1) says, 'is woven into the complex tapestry of people's lives. People make pottery vessels and then distribute, use, break and discard them in the archaeological record all in the context of their everyday life'. It is 'one of the oldest activities of humankind' (Cooper 2000 p. 6); 'mankind's oldest art discipline' (Clark 2017, p. 4). In many ways it's unsurprising, then, that archaeologists have a lead start on researchers of world politics when it comes to studying ceramics. That's because it lasts a really long time; pottery dating back to prehistoric times is 'one of the most frequently recovered artifacts, and it has remarkable preservation once broken into sherds' (Skibo 1994, p. 1).[4] 'It is striking', Neil MacGregor notes, 'that when a plate or a vase is whole it is alarmingly fragile; once it

50 *Ceramics*

is smashed the pieces of pottery are almost indestructible' (2012, p. 327). Pottery also survives remarkably well underwater; while textiles and spices were also things commonly shipped around the world, they didn't stand the test of time if the ship sank. Ceramics, however, did – to the extent that 'shipwreck pottery' has been used to accurately date mystery shipwrecks. 'Ceramic survives', as Paul Greenhalgh (2017, p. 25) tells us; '[e]ventually it becomes the only thing that means anything in a culture'.

We can study clay from a dizzying array of perspectives – tell all sorts of different stories – including about its history, its material properties, manufacturing processes, the uses of pottery, the economics of the production and distribution of pottery, how vessels have been used over time, how pots have been decorated, the chemistry of pottery and so on (see Rice 2005 [1987]). Archaeologists, ethnographers, historians, scientists, anthropologists, and, of course, artists have all laid claim to ceramics as a research topic.

It's interesting, then, that IR scholars haven't tried to get a slice of the ceramics pie, because clay and ceramics are very much present in world politics when you look for them. Unmined clay helped the Viet Cong build sturdy tunnels, which contributed to their thwarting the Americans in the Vietnam War (Bardgett 2017). Clay mining has a significant detrimental impact on the environment (Mukherjee 2013) and – like most mining activities – also raises serious questions about the labour conditions and human rights of the miners (Human Rights Watch 2020). There are gender politics of clay, and of clay mining (Birch Aguilar 2007; Lahiri-Dutt and Burke 2011), and a political economy to ceramics (see Greene 2012); porcelain was widely traded between Europe and China as far back as the 1500s (Ostermann 2006, p. 81), Brazilian immigrants revived an ailing tile industry in Portugal in the late nineteenth century (Ostermann 2006, p. 79), and ceramics continue to be bought and sold in lucrative international markets, including in renowned auction houses, such as Sotheby's, Bonhams, and Christie's. They are also popular, often portable, very evocative mementoes of a particular place, meaning that there can be a significant tourist economy associated with them (see Scheid 2015). Ceramics, like other forms of cultural heritage, have been used 'to transmit orthodox national history narratives and to establish national identities' (Bennett 2012, p. 37). They have 'become part of an international language [and] … ceramists in many countries have retained aspects of identifiable styles, which though far from being nationalistic celebrate cultural and national difference' (Cooper 2000, p. 333).

Ceramics also play a role in everyday political practice; they are a means of bringing people together and building communities. They are used to destigmatise abortion by promoting compassion, in the case of Plants for

Ceramics 51

Patients (plantsforpatients.org/), where those who have had an abortion are offered a plant in a handmade pot accompanied by a handwritten note of support. Ceramic artists have also come together to auction their work and raise money to support survivors of natural disasters such as the 2015 earthquake in Nepal (see Australian Ceramics 2015) and the Australian bushfires in 2020 (Herbert 2020). Ceramics are a means through which rural Nicaraguan potters can express and sustain their heritage while earning an income; and through which dirty water can be made safe to drink, by training local potters to make ceramic water filters – two projects run by Potters for Peace/Ceramistas por la Paz (n.d.; see also Potters without Borders [n.d.] on ceramic water filters).

Beyond this, ceramics can see humble plates turned into biting social commentaries; salt and pepper shakers transformed into shocking representations of some of the key events of the twentieth century; and soap dishes become powerful proclamations of anti-war sentiment. As we will soon see, there is much, much more to the humble ceramic than first meets the eye.

Bringing politics to the (kitchen) table

Plates, salt and pepper shakers, and soap dishes tend to be things that we might think of as peripheral, if relevant at all, to world politics. Their production and circulation, as noted above, have political economic implications, and you might expect to see some fancy dinnerware at a state banquet. But beyond that, we don't treat these artefacts as the site of world politics; we don't interrogate them in the way we do more conventional political artefacts. This is because, much like my discussion of textiles, we don't expect to see calls to arms in the form of little porcelain statuettes or political messages on dinner plates; a tea set conventionally understood is not a site in which we expect to find (or, more accurately, look for) world politics. We have not been taught to search for politics on or around the kitchen table. And yet,

> [f]rom the glazed brick and tiled mosques of Persia to the royal commemorative ware of the European monarchies to the blue and white delftware celebrating the growth of colonial trade, ceramics have been used to normalize dominant political ideologies by means of ordinary, everyday things.
>
> (Clare 2016, p. 35)

Equally, the form has been used by 'revolutionary and oppositionist movements ... to overturn the process by using commonplace ceramic objects to project their visions, articulate their ideologies and agitate among the

52 *Ceramics*

masses' (Clare 2006, p. 35). There are politics to be found, then, everywhere we look.

Roberto Lugo explores the disjuncture of big politics featuring on everyday ceramics in his *To Disarm* (2020) series (see Wexler Gallery n.d.). Lugo is an artist and a self-described 'ghetto potter' (Goyanes 2017) whose ceramic work focuses on power and injustice, and comes in the form of busts, urns, bowls, and teapots. *To Disarm* (2020) is a set of teapots of varying size and shape, though all of fairly conventional design, made of the usual ceramic, China paint, enamel, epoxy ... and gun parts, including triggers as handles and gun barrels for spouts. So, not your average afternoon tea. On the body of the teapot, Lugo depicts prominent Black and Latino figures: bell hooks and Celia Cruz share one teapot, Biggie and Harriet Tubman another, and Angela Davis and John Lewis a third. Other teapots variously feature explorer Matthew Henson, novelist Ralph Ellison, and John Lewis, the politician and civil rights leader, amongst others. As Lugo (2020) explains, having your face painted on a teapot was once the domain of the rich and the privileged; it was a sign of high status. In contrast, in Lugo's words,

> The portraits I chose for these works are mugshots of Civil Rights leaders, and other cultural figures representative of Black and Latino culture. Their likeness is elevated to a space that was historically inaccessible to people of color, stripping the teapot of its Euro-centric roots.

Simultaneously, the guns represent 'gun violence, which disproportionately affects communities of color, resulting in death and incarceration at rates higher than the national average' (Lugo 2020). In addition to being visually striking, then, these teapots are rich in meaning, canvassing representation, recognition, subjugation, and violence.[5]

Lugo's series has a similar effect as Marianne Jørgensen's tank blanket that I discussed in Chapter 3, and Nancy Meli Walker's necklace, *War and Peace Choke Her*, which I looked at in Chapter 4. What's happening here, when we bring together one of the most destructive elements of public life with one of the most quotidian? What does it mean to place the warmth, the cosiness, the comfort, of a blanket or a pot of tea, flush up against the cold, hard metal of weaponry? For me, it offers a stark comment on the militarisation of the everyday. Military culture and aesthetic pervades our everyday lives in all sorts of invisibilised ways (see Enloe 2000 and Åhäll 2015), from clothes (see, for example, Shepherd 2018 on 'military chic') to toys and games (Stahl 2006) and beyond. It has become normalised; we don't do a double-take when we see someone wearing a pair of cargo pants or a 'bomber' jacket. It is only when something even more

Ceramics 53

innocuous, and purportedly distanced from politics, becomes militarised that we even see it. Plates and tea services – so often the domain of cakes and miniature forks, a break over a cup of tea, or a meal marking the end of a workday – are so thoroughly part of the private, the domestic, and the invisible, that it almost seems absurd to see politics in and on them. And therein lies the power.

Same, too, with soap dishes. Theories of global politics don't tell us to go looking for soap dishes, nor do the methods that we're taught to study the world equip us to deal with this artefact. And yet, failing to look for politics in soap dishes means that we miss Walter Ostrom's Iraqi War soap dishes, which would be a shame indeed, as they offer powerful critiques of the 2003 invasion of Iraq and ensuing occupation. Made of thrown and press-moulded earthenware, featuring a maiolica glaze and painted stains, and inspired by Italian *istoriato* imagery,[6] Ostrom's soap dishes follow in the footsteps of 'a long and rich tradition of commemorative ceramics' (Ostrom in Ostermann 2006, p. 197). He made them to address his feelings of helplessness as the world watched the US-led invasion and accompanying bombastic rhetoric. The pair of soap dishes that make up *Iraqi War Soap Dishes*, 2003 – which started Ostrom's *Lady Macbeth* series ('dealing with all those events that white liberals would like to wash off their hands' [Ostrom in Ostermann 2006, p. 197]) – feature very traditional imagery. Upon closer inspection, though, the decorative ribbons, in cornflower blue and a muted yellow, feature the date of invasion (19 March 2003), and identify Blair and Bush as the 'Axis of Evil'. The scales of justice depicted on the top of one soap dish is unbalanced, and the two Lady Justices that flank either side of this piece are tightly bound. In the middle, the world cracks and burns. The second soap dish features a weeping willow – another '[symbol] of disaster and death' (Ostrom in Ostermann 2006, pp. 197–198). Invasion, conflict, death, guilt, injustice, complicity … all on a humble soap dish.

Then we have Paul Mathieu's salt and pepper shakers, *S & P Shakers (Disasters)*. Mathieu has captured many high profile international political events of the twentieth century – '20th century disasters' (Mathieu 2000) – in shaker-form. Concentration camps are there (Mathieu 1999/2000a), as are the assassination of John F. Kennedy (including a tiny, clambering, pink-suited Jackie Kennedy) (Mathieu 1999/2000b), the Oklahoma City bombing (Mathieu 1999/2000c), and the Oka crisis (Mathieu 1999/2000d). The one I keep coming back to, though, is the pair of World Trade Center shakers (Mathieu 2002 – see Figure 5.1). I'm sure that part of my fascination with this piece comes from the fact that it is one of the only pieces of the series that commemorates an event I was aware of happening in real time; a couple of weeks shy of my fifteenth birthday, I remember going

54 *Ceramics*

Figure 5.1 Paul Mathieu, *W.T.C. 9-11, 2001*, 2002. Source: Copyright Paul Mathieu, reproduced with the permission of Paul Mathieu.

through to the living room to say goodnight to my dad, and together we stared in horror as the news from New York unravelled before us. And so, while the scale, violence, and death toll of the Holocaust, and the atomic bombs dropped on Hiroshima and Nagasaki (which are also fashioned out of clay – see Mathieu 1999/2000e) far exceed that of 11 September 2001, the former remains especially arresting to me.

Converting the Twin Towers (once the tallest towers in the world), the two planes that flew into them, and the resulting explosions into something small – holdable – is part of it. This scaling down works in a similar way as the little arpillera figures and the scaled-down jewellery rocket launchers. Making big things small makes them more perceptible (see also Stewart 2003); the sheer scale of 9/11 – and, indeed, Hiroshima, Nagasaki, and the Holocaust – renders it almost outside of knowability, outside of true comprehension. But making miniature the big makes the abstract less abstract and somehow drives home the horror more acutely. The World Trade Center shakers also freeze history in a point of time – a sort of temporal liminal space in which we collectively held our breaths; in which the towers still stood; in which we grappled with the concept of a plane (let alone

Figure 5.2 Penny Byrne, *Sands of Gallipoli (Gallipoli Porn?)* (2015). Repurposed vintage ceramic urn, donated ANZAC Day badges, collected ANZAC Day memorabilia, Rising Sun hat badge, miniature Gallipoli Campaign Service medals, paper collage, emu feathers, ANZAC Day Poppies, custom plinth, PVA, epoxy resin. H × 1900mm W × 700mm D × 330mm. Source: Photograph by Matthew Stanton. Copyright: Penny Byrne, reproduced with the permission of Penny Byrne.

two planes) flying into a skyscraper. The use of clay may be an uncomfortably apt material, representing the fragility and temporariness of the period between the planes hitting and the towers collapsing. And, of course, there's the artefactuality of these pieces – salt and pepper shakers,[7] sitting as they do in the middle of the symbolic heart of the home, the kitchen table. It is subversive;

> The innocent, familiar, functional, decorative and commemorative format of the salt and pepper shakers reinforces our ambiguous relation to these events and brings them subversively into our homes and our daily lives. This reaffirms the need never to forget that remembrance and memory must follow us even in the most ordinary and domestic circumstances.
>
> (Mathieu in Ostermann 2006, p. 199)

56 *Ceramics*

All of these domestic ceramic artefacts act as souvenirs of things we would rather forget – and I use 'souvenirs' here in the literal sense of 'remember-ings' (from the French 'souvenir' meaning 'memory' or 'remembrance'). We can remember these events on marked days with ceremonies and speeches and schedules. There is a place for that. But how powerful for us to reflect on the decisions made in our names in the quiet everyday. To reflect on the people killed, and wars waged, in the name of our protection; and to think – deeply – about the world that we want to inhabit. As we make a pot of tea or wash our hands. As we sit around the kitchen table with loved ones. World politics aren't divorced from our lives, these artefacts say; and nor are our lives divorced from world politics.

Kneading new stories[8]

Ehren Tool served as a US Marine, taking part in the Gulf War and then serving as an Embassy Guard (Tool 2018). After he was discharged, he took a ceramics class at a community college and started making cups. Not just any cups, mind – these are 'brutal-looking clay stoneware cups that he decorates with images about war – cups that he hopes will start hon-est conversations about war and the conflicted, complicated feelings and experiences that come with it' (Brice 2020). Nearly 22,000 cups on (Brice 2020), Tool is doing precisely this. Insignias, flags, and skulls are stamped into some of the cups, while snipers peer through gun-sights on others; on one, the Grim Reaper rises out of a jumble of skeletons and darkly thanks veterans for their service. Tool has sent cups to 'national and corporate heads urging them to consider the outcome of supporting continued war efforts' (Ceramics Now 2019), while also making cups for veterans and their families. Tool's work, then, represents resistance against a sort of casual militarisation; he wants us to know how dark war is for the human beings at the frontlines.

Tool's first solo exhibition, 'Production or Destruction' of 2012, show-cased 1,000 of his cups. The cups – which 'have been called [Tool's] sol-diers' (Tool n.d.) – were exhibited 'in "units" based on military formations of "squads" (13), "platoons" (55), and "companies" (225)' (Ceramics Now 2019). It has echoes of Tool's earlier installation piece, *393* (2004), which 'is a striking display of 393 shattered cups that represent the number of US combat casualties during the first year of the second Gulf War' (Ceramics Now 2019). Some of the cups are still standing but most lie in pile of sherds, no longer functional. There is something especially poignant about this piece. Militaries, after all, are designed to homogenise a group; individual-ity is dissuaded if not entirely suppressed (see Nate Powell's brilliant 2019 piece 'About Face' on the regulation of soldiers' physical appearance for

Ceramics 57

just one example).[9] Tool's cups represent this homogeneity; and the broken ones, of course, represent the shattered lives, marked by death and trauma. The cups therefore simultaneously represent and unsettle this homogenisation, and remind us that underneath all of the camouflage are very breakable, and sometimes un-put-back-together-able, bodies. 'They may be more than [just] cups', Tool concedes (Tool 2018).

And like the plates and teapots above, cups are very, invisibly, innocuously everyday. We don't ask cups to make grand anti-war statements, or to shift the way we think about militaries, conflicts, and violence. 'Nobody expects cups to do that', Tool says; '[t]hey almost have no cultural weight' (Tool in Jao 2012). And again, it is in their scale, their domesticity, and their so-everyday-we-don't-even-see-them-anymore-ness that these cups pack their punch. The 'beauty and delicacy' (Jao 2012) of Tool's pieces only serve to underline the horror and brutality of war, and of the collusion(s) and collision(s) of military and civilian life (Tool n.d.). This is what drives his art: 'I would like my work to vindicate the principles of peace and justice in the world. That is a lot to ask of a cup' (Tool n.d.).

Tool's work therefore represents resistance against manufactured sameness; another set of artefacts – the results of Joel Pfeiffer's 'clay stomps' – represents resistance against manufactured difference, and also serves to underscore the affective aspect of pottery which I haven't really explored so far. Pfeiffer's first 'clay stomp' took place in 1974, and came about because buying pre-mixed clay was more expensive than simply buying some powdered clay, adding some water, and inviting a few neighbours over to get stomping. Since then, Pfeiffer has led over a hundred stomps, the resulting clay of which has been used in murals that are now installed in public libraries, schools, and art museums. One of these stomps – the American/Soviet Clay Stomp – took place on 11 June 1989, in Milwaukee, Wisconsin. More than 5,000 people mixed eight tons of clay, which was then used to make a ceramic mural, *Clay: A Healing Way*, with a central theme of peace and connection. Just a few months later, the mural – all 342 square feet of it – was flown to (what was then) Leningrad, where several thousand Russians had had a reciprocal clay stomping session, which resulted in a second peace mural – this one destined for Milwaukee (Heart Roots Art n.d.).

Pfeiffer's clay stomps actively incorporate the preparation and the process into the artefact that is produced. It isn't just the end product that matters; the journey from powder to clay to ceramic panel to mural is a process that imbues the artefact with a particular and additional meaning. Usually, we just get the story of the final artefact – the pot that has already been painted, say, or the woven weaving. In the case of the American/Soviet Clay Stomp, the preparation process and the physicality of the making are intrinsic to the murals' meaning (much like colcha embroidery). It is

58 *Ceramics*

meaning-making in the most literal sense. The clay was prepared during the Cold War, with a spirit of reciprocity and a shared desire for peace in mind. The stomps also point to the power of making, and of making collaboratively. Pfeiffer reports that one of his Russian friends reflected that, 'As we mix the clay, the clay mixes us' (Lantern 2019). The stomps bring people together in the same way that it brings the clay together, and connects sometimes unlikely groups of people – such as American and Russians in 1989. In 1993, Pfeiffer explained that '[t]he goal of this whole project is world peace ... I know that's a lofty thought, but it all starts with one step, or one stomp' (Lantern 2019).

The work of another ceramic artist, Penny Byrne (see https://pennybyrneartist.com/), tells stories about all sorts of political things. Her *#EuropaEuropa* (2015) series, a commentary on the perilous journeys undertaken by asylum seekers and restrictive border control policies, is made up of dozens of delicate vintage porcelain figurines atop an antique serving platter. All of the figures are in dainty period costumes (think bonnets with ribbons, parasols, and waistcoats with pantaloons) with Byrne's addition of lurid orange life vests around each of their necks. Her work has commented on everything from Australia's appalling treatment of Indigenous Australians (*Mission Statement – Sorry*, 2008), to the effects of global warming (*Not a Glimmer of Hope,* 2010) and Donald Trump (*Putin's Poodle*, 2017). It has also prompted a consideration of the ways in which we commemorate military events, as in *Sands of Gallipoli (Gallipoli Porn?)* (2015) (see Figure 5.2), in which Byrne repurposed a vintage ceramic urn and adorned it with all sorts of ANZAC Day tchotchkes.

Byrne's work blends humour with biting political commentary, partly by virtue of the dissonance between the source material (the figurines) and the end product. *In Happier Times (Gaddafi and his Gal Guards Guarding Gaddafi)* (2011) is a good example of this, as well as of how making politics in miniature can be extraordinarily powerful. Muammar Gaddafi was known for his elite cadre of female bodyguards – known as The Revolutionary Nuns (Flock 2011).[10] Byrne has reproduced this set-up, with eight figurines (now toting an admirable selection of weapons, and their dainty dresses now camouflaged in khaki) flanking a parodically tall, tiny-mouthed, sunglasses-wearing, bejewelled-sash-adorned Gaddafi. But Byrne has retained hints of the figurines' past lives; a placid lamb sits at the feet of one of the 'Gal Guards', staring up lovingly at its rouged-cheeked owner; another of the guards sits primly on an ornate chair while her colleague – a former ballerina, if the tutu is anything to go by – points her tiny ceramic toes in a tiny pair of black ceramic ballet slippers surrounded by flowers in pastel shades; and Gaddafi still holds onto a blue bonnet in his right hand – a relic from a past ceramic life.

And it makes sense for Gaddafi to be represented in this way. As James Delingpole (2014) reflected,

> Sure, we'd all heard about the funny stuff: the time John Simpson went to see him and he farted noisily (Gaddafi, not Simpson) through the interview; the ridiculous outfits; the bullet-proof Bedouin-style tent that he insisted on bringing on his last world tour, complete with live camels to graze decoratively outside.

But this veneer of a sort of charming eccentricity – of which his glamourous female guards were undoubtedly a part – distracted from the reality of Gaddafi as 'ferocious tyrant' (Spencer 2011), a 'dictator capable of ... barbarities' (Delingpole 2014). The original form of the figurine, Byrne's assiduous attention to detail and the juxtaposition of coy and coiffed young women bearing automatic guns, grenades, missiles, and knives all add up to grimly underscore the duality of Gaddafi himself.

Conclusion

I'll be honest, when I started this research, I didn't expect to find myself in the world of teapots, salt and pepper shakers, and cups. Much like Cynthia Enloe once said, few social scientists were 'initially attracted to their professions by images of themselves taking notes in a brothel, a kitchen, or a latrine' (2011, p. 447) – or, indeed, 'households, assembly lines, sweat shops, farms, secretariats, [and] guerrilla wars' (Bleiker 2000, p. 8). Finding out just how political these ceramics are came as something of a surprise to me, because we don't go about our daily business expecting a teapot to teach us about race; or for soap dishes to make powerful comment on the illegal invasion of a country; or for tiny dictators to turn up as figurines wearing a bonnet. And when we do see these stories, they are so angry and clever and sardonic and healing and unexpected and complex. They're somehow simultaneously *funny* and utterly grim. They are shocking, and they make you want to share them with someone else. They are remarkable stories, and remarkable everyday artefacts of world politics.

Notes

1 I use 'ceramics' and 'pottery' interchangeably in this chapter, as per common usage, and take my lead from the makers that I discuss as to what kind of maker they are. This is because it's quite tricky – '[t]he practitioners may be designated potters, studio potters, cerami(ci)sts, ceramic artists, clay artists, artists, craftspeople or makers. The names are not innocent. They have a history and carry a trail of associations' (Vincentelli 2017, p. 342). But it is worth noting that

60 *Ceramics*

pottery is a term that refers to a specific kind of ceramics; one that is generally concerned with the making of containers or vessels (as in, the 'pot' in 'pottery') using clay and clay alone. Pots are ceramics, but so too are bricks, pipes, and tiles, as well as dental implants, cooktops, and skis.

2 For a truly stunning piece of writing on porcelain, you can't go past Edmund de Waal's *The White Road* (2015), which is a globetrotting love letter to porcelain.

3 Pigments and glazes, too, have specific geographies; a certain glaze used by some Japanese potters came from Chinese cobalt – 'ground up dark green asbolite pebbles from [Chinese] riverbeds, which contain 10-30% of cobalt oxide as well as silica and many other chemicals' (Rawson 1971, p. 55; see also Leach 2011, p. 129).

4 The terms 'sherds' and 'shards' are somewhat interchangeable – archaeologists tend to speak of 'sherds' specifically in the context of pottery, while the rest of us go with 'shards', but essentially, we're all talking about the same thing: a bit of broken, sharp-edged material that you don't want to stand on.

5 See also Dr Sarah Laurenson's (2018) reflections on The Empire Café tea set, recently acquired by the National Museum of Scotland, and which critically explores links between Scotland and the transatlantic slave trade.

6 As Ostermann (2006, p. 65) explains: 'Perhaps the best-known tin-glazed ceramics of the Italian Renaissance are the narrative *istoriato* (story) wares, which came into being during the early 1500s. In earlier maiolica wares there had been a union of shape and decoration secondary to the actual function of the piece (serving dishes, jars, ewers, drug pots, and so on). *Istoriato* wares were a departure from this – they were conceived primarily as vehicles for painted stories, and hence shallow and open-surfaced dishes were favoured as shapes to best present narratives.'

7 Salt and pepper shakers themselves have a political history; as Derek Workman (2012) explains, 'it was the Great Depression of the 1930s that gave a major boost to the popularity of salt and pepper shakers as both a household and collectible item. Ceramics producers worldwide were forced to restrict production and concentrate on lower-priced items; an obvious product was the salt and pepper shaker. Bright and cheery, it could be bought for a few cents at most local hardware stores. Soon other ceramics companies got into the act. Japanese firms had a large share of the market from the late 1920s through the 1930s, as well as from the late 1940s through the 1950s. (Production was halted during World War II.) The shakers they produced in the postwar years, labeled "Made in occupied Japan," or simply "Occupied Japan," are extremely rare and highly sought after'. Collectors of these artefacts are not messing around; there are museums (https://www.thesaltandpeppershakermuseum.com), identification and value guides (see, for example, Florence 2002), and clubs with newsletters (https://www.saltandpepperclub.com).

8 Kneading clay is akin to kneading dough, and is done for the purpose of getting air bubbles out and making it more durable. I've been told that puns don't work if they have to be explained, but I think this one is good enough to withstand a brief explanatory footnote.

9 With many thanks to Nicole Wegner for sharing Powell's work with me.

10 Former bodyguards have since told of the coercion and sexual violence that marked their employ with Gaddafi (see Flock 2011).

6 A short reflection on everyday artefacts of world politics (and all the other questions I still have)

So, there we have it: three kinds of everyday artefacts of world politics. In textiles, jewellery, and ceramics lies the world of world politics. Through these things, everyday people tell stories of colonialism, conquest, and violence; and stories of beauty, colour, joy, and celebration. There are stories of identity and protest, of transformation and place, and of subversion and resistance. Some of the stories cover ground familiar to IR, while other stories tell more personal stories: of finding one's place in the world, and of reflecting on life experiences. But they are all stories of world politics; everyday stories, told through things, about how the world works (or, at least, how the world should, or could, work).

This is an apt place to wrap up this present story but, as is often the case, there is *more* story to tell. Really, there's a second half to this story. In this book, I have focused almost exclusively on the artefacts. The makers are there, but they stand a little bit behind the artefacts; my spotlight has been closely trained on the things, and not on the people that made the things. But I am nonetheless curious. I want to know these makers better. Who are they? What does their everyday look like? Why do they make? Where, and how, and what do they make? Do they *feel* like they are making political things? Indeed, do they feel like actors of world politics? *What are their stories?*

And then, beyond the makers, I have many questions about making. *Why* do we make? What do we do when we make something? Does our drive come from the 'wellspring of spiritual fulfillment' that comes from 'think[ing] the world into being for oneself' (Korn 2017 [2013], p. 8)? A feeling of 'flow' (Csikszentmihalyi 1990)? As Edmund de Waal says, on making pottery, 'I'm in this moment while also being elsewhere. Altogether elsewhere' (2015, p. 4). Is making in our blood? Were we perhaps made to make?:

> You and I and everyone you know are descended from tens of thousands of years of makers. Decorators, tinkerers, storytellers, dancers,

DOI: 10.4324/9781003122340-6

62   *A short reflection*

explorers, fiddlers, drummers, builders, grows, problem-solvers, and embellishers – these are our common ancestors.

(Gilbert 2015, p. 89)

For me, at least, it feels akin to magic, to summon up something from nothing, the knowledge that this *thing* would not be here without my having made it; 'some entirely unique, inimitable thing that didn't exist just a couple of hours ago, and which I have brought into existence myself ... this is my daily magic' (Baume 2020, p. 183). As Matthew B. Crawford (2009, p. 15) puts it, there's a 'satisfaction of manifesting oneself concretely in the world through manual competence', and as David Esterly says: 'Idea in mind, brush or pen or chisel in hand, you begin to fancy that you're creating something that was meant to exist, that exists before you make it' (2015 [2013], p. 54). And there is also a sense of leaving a legacy in my makings: when I go, I will have left things behind that only I could have made – 'a material testimonial of ... [my] curiosity and investigation', in the words of Sara Baume (2020, p. 36). A crocheted cactus as a housewarming gift. A tiny navy-blue knitted cardigan to welcome a new baby. My wonky handmade ceramic bowls. This book.

Through my discussion of textiles, jewellery, and ceramics, I have pointed to very tangible, empirical examples of things already *made*. But surely the theory – and, perhaps, the feeling – of making also has something to teach International Relations. After all, world politics has always been a place of making of sorts; foreign policies are made, as are agreements. People make war, and also make peace. Actors in world politics can make threats, or make promises, or try 'to make the world a less bloody place' (Gowan 2014). Alliances are made, just as enemies are made. The more idealistic might dream of making a difference; global corporations would probably prefer to make money. Policymakers make lots of things: policies and speeches; resolutions, laws, and memoranda; judgements and announcements. So too do theory makers, who make journal articles, books and essays, analyses and commentaries. Can making world politics differently encourage us to make different world politics?

There are a few reasons why I think the idea of *making* world politics might offer some interesting thought prompts (see also Tidy 2019). First, if we make world politics, we can remake them, and unmake them. There is a fundamentally political aspect to making; how we choose to make things involves choices that, at their heart, have politics. As Elaine Lipson (2012, pp. 10–11) explains:

Opting to make things in a conscientious and authentic way becomes a political act and an optimistic vote for a sustainable world when you contrast it with a world where few people know how to make anything with their hands; where we are consumers but not creators; where our

A short reflection   63

choices are determined by a conflux of corporate interests that run big-box stores fuelled by multinational manufacturing where the cheapest, most polluting and most inhumane methods rule the day.

While Lipson was talking about craft and the politics of production, her ideas relate very much to the responsibility we have, as IR scholars, to think very carefully about the sort of world that we are crafting (as Smith 2004 also urges).

Embracing this idea of making world politics also means that policy-makers and theory makers, along with the everyday makers that featured in this book, together constitute a community of makers – and one of story-tellers – all of whom make the ideas and the artefacts that make up world politics. While the former two overwhelmingly use words to make their ideas and artefacts, everyday making draws from a much broader variety of constitutive ingredients: clay, ink, thread and wool, pixels, sounds, and precious stones to name just some. If we reframe *doing* politics as *making* politics – continuously crafting world affairs – it not only shifts the ideas we have about world politics; it also opens up our thinking about what the artefacts of world politics can be, which then opens up questions about how politics can be made and about who can make politics.

But the answers to these questions are not for the present story; they will need to come later. The point of sneaking these early thoughts about making into the conclusion is to show that there are many, many more stories to tell about the everyday artefacts of world politics, and just as many ways to tell these stories. But I think it is worth doing so, not least because it might inspire us to consider whether there are different ways of making the world, and making world politics; ones that are more inclusive, and more just for all.

But again, these are stories for another time. For now, it is enough to say that everyday people tell stories about how the world works through the things they make. And we should pay attention to these things – to this *stuff* of world politics – for it lets us understand how world politics are lived, and made, everywhere and every day.

Bibliography

Acuto, Michele (2014) 'Everyday international relations: Garbage, grand designs, and mundane matters', *International Political Sociology*, 8: 345–362.

Adams, Jacqueline (2012) 'Exiles, art, and political activism: Fighting the Pinochet regime from afar', *Journal of Refugee Studies*, 26(3): 436–457.

Adichie, Chimamanda Ngozi (2009) 'The danger of a single story', *TED*, October 2009, http://www.ted.com/talks/chimamanda_adichie_the_danger_of_a_singl e_story/transcript?language=en

Agathangelou, Anna M. and L.H.M. Ling (2009) *Transforming World Politics: From Empire to Multiple Worlds*, London and New York: Routledge.

Agosín, Marjorie (1996) *Tapestries of Hope, Threads of Love: The Arpillera Movement in Chile, 1974–1994*, USA: Rowman & Littlefield Publishers.

Åhäll, Linda (2015) 'The hidden politics of militarization and pop culture as political communication', pp. 63–72 in Federica Caso and Caitlin Hamilton (eds) *Popular Culture and World Politics: Theories, Methods, Pedagogies*, Bristol: E-IR Publishing.

Åhäll, Linda and Stefan Borg (2013) 'Predication, presupposition and subject-positioning', pp. 196–207 in Laura J. Shepherd (ed.) *Critical Approaches to Security: An Introduction to Theories and Methods*, London and New York: Routledge.

Åhäll, Linda and Thomas Gregory (eds) (2015) *Emotions, Politics and War*, Oxon and New York: Routledge.

Ailes, Emma (2013) 'The making of the Great Tapestry of Scotland', *BBC News*, 3 September 2013, http://www.bbc.com/news/uk-scotland-23935135

Anand, Anita (2016) 'The Koh-i-Noor diamond is in Britain illegally. But it should still stay there', *The Guardian*, 16 February 2016, https://www.theguardian.com/ commentisfree/2016/feb/16/koh-i-noor-diamond-britain-illegally-india-pakistan -afghanistan-history-tower

Andersen, Rune S., Juha A. Viori and Xavier Guillaume (2015) 'Chromatology of security: Introducing colours to visual security studies', *Security Dialogue*, 46(5): 440–457.

66 Bibliography

Ändra, Christine, Berit Bliesemann de Guevara, Lydia Cole and Danielle House (2020) 'Knowing through needlework: Curating the difficult knowledge of conflict textiles', *Critical Military Studies*, 6(3–4): 341–359.

Andrew, Sonja (2008) 'Textile semantics: Considering a communication-based reading of textiles', *Textile: The Journal of Cloth and Culture*, 6(1): 32–65.

Appadurai, Arjun (2013) 'Introduction: Commodities and the politics of value', pp. 1–63 in Arjun Appadurai (ed.) *The Social Life of Things: Commodities in Cultural Perspective*, UK: Cambridge University Press.

Appadurai, Arjun (ed.) (2013) *The Social Life of Things: Commodities in Cultural Perspective*, UK: Cambridge University Press.

Areo, Margaret Olugbemisola and Abedowale Biodun Areo (2012) 'Textiles, political propaganda, and the economic implications in Southwestern Nigeria', Textile Society of America Symposium Proceedings, paper 657, http://digitalc ommons.unl.edu/cgi/viewcontent.cgi?article=1656&context=tsaconf

Art Gallery of Ontario (2001) 'Barb Hunt: Antipersonnel', http://www.ago.net/barb -hunt

Asante-Kyei, Kofi and Alexander Addae (2016) 'The economic and environmental impacts on clay harvesting at Abonko in the Mfantsiman West District of Central Region, Ghana', *American Scientific Research Journal for Engineering, Technology, and Sciences (ASRJETS)*, 18(1): 120–132.

Auslander, Leora (2005) 'Beyond words', *American Historical Review*, 110(4): 1015–1045.

Australian Ceramics (2015) 'Ceramic artists raise over $40,000 for Nepal', https:/ /www.australianceramics.com/2015/05/18/ceramic-artists-raise-over-40000-for -nepal.

Australian Women's Archives Project (2013) 'Parliament House embroidery' http:// www.womenaustralia.info/biogs/AWE4886b.htm

Autessere, Séverine (2014) *Peaceland: Conflict Resolution and the Everyday Politics of International Intervention*, New York: Cambridge University Press.

Ayres, Ed (2019) 'More than bling – Su san Cohn makes jewellery with a political message', *The Art Show*, https://www.abc.net.au/radionational/programs/the-art -show/susan-cohn-jeweller/11474978

Barkham, Patrick (2011) 'Nazis, needlework and my dad', *The Guardian*, 3 September 2011, http://www.theguardian.com/lifeandstyle/2011/sep/03/tony -casdagli-father-stitching-nazis.

Barlo, Stuart, William (Bill) Edgar Boyd, Alessandro Pelizzon, and Shawn Wilson (2020) 'Yarning as protected space: Principles and protocols', *AlterNative: An Internatonal Journal of Indigenous Peoples*, 16(2): 90–98.

Barrett, Michael (2019) 'Three years after Denmark's infamous 'jewellery law' hit world headlines, not a single piece has been confiscated', *The Local*, https://ww w.thelocal.dk/20190124/three-years-after-denmarks-infamous-jewellery-law-hit -world-headlines-not-a-single-piece-has-been-confiscated

Barthes, Roland (2009 [1957]) *Mythologies*, translated by A. Lavers, London: Paladin.

Baume, Sara (2020) *Handiwork*, Dublin: Tramp Press.

Bibliography 67

BBC News (2016) 'Laos: Barack Obama regrets 'biggest bombing in history'', 7 September 2016, https://www.bbc.com/news/world-asia-37286520

Bean, Susan S. (2015) 'Gandhi and khadi, the fabric of Indian independence', pp. 234–246 in Jessica Hemmings (ed.) *The Textile Reader*, London and New York: Bloomsbury Academic.

Bennett, Gwen (2012) 'National history and identity narratives in the People's Republic of China', pp. 37–56 in Charles W. Hartley, G. Bike Yazicioğlu and Adam T. Smith (eds) *The Archaeology of Power and Politics in Eurasia*, London: Cambridge University Press.

Bennett, Jane (2009) *Vibrant Matter: A Political Ecology of Things*, Duke Univerrsity Press.

Bardgett, Richard (2017) 'In war, the earth matters', *OUPblog*, https://blog.oup.com/2017/03/war-earth-soil-matters/

Berents, Helen (2018) *Young People and Everyday Peace: Exclusion, Insecurity and Peacebuilding in Colombia*, New York and London: Routledge.

Bessarab, Dawn and Bridget Ng'andu (2010) 'Yarning about yarning as a legitimate method in Indigenous research', *International Journal of Critical Indigenous Studies*, 3(1): 37–50, https://ijcis.qut.edu.au/article/view/57/57

Birch Aguilar, Laurel (2007) 'Metaphors, myths and making pots: Chewa clay arts', *African Arts*, 40(1): 64–70.

Björkdahl, Annika, Martin Hall and Ted Svensson (2019) 'Everyday international relations: Editors' introduction', *Cooperation and Conflict*, 54(2): 123–130.

Black, Anthea and Nicole Burisch (2011) 'Craft hard die free: Radical curatorial strategies for craftivism', pp. 204–221 in Maria Elena Buszek (ed.) *Extra/Ordinary: Craft and Contemporary Art*, Durham and London: Duke University Press.

Bleiker, Roland (1997) 'Forget IR theory', *Alternatives: Global, Local, Political*, 22(1): 57–85.

Bleiker, Roland (2000) *Popular Dissent, Human Agency, and Global Politics*, Cambridge: Cambridge University Press.

Bleiker, Roland (2001) 'The aesthetic turn in international political theory', *Millennium: Journal of International Studies*, 30(3): 509–533.

Bleiker, Roland (2009) *Aesthetics and World Politics*, Basingstoke and New York: Palgrave Macmillan.

Bleiker, Roland (2015) 'Pluralist methods for visual global politics', *Millennium: Journal of International Studies*, 43(3): 872–890.

Boissoneault, Lorraine (2017) 'The true story of the Koh-i-Noor Diamond – and why the British won't give it back', *Smithsonian Magazine*, https://www.smithsonianmag.com/history/true-story-koh-i-noor-diamondand-why-british-wont-give-it-back-180964660/

Brice, Anne (2020) 'Ehren Tool's cups aren't for sale. They're for starting conversations – about war', *Berkeley News*, 20 February 2020, https://news.berkeley.edu/2020/02/20/ehren-tool-war-cups/

Briggs, Morgan and Roland Bleiker (2010) 'Authoethnographic International Relations: Exploring the self as a source of knowledge', *Review of International Studies*, 36: 779–798.

68 Bibliography

Brinkman, Svend (2012) *Qualitative Inquiry in Everyday Life*, London: SAGE Publications.

Bristow, Maxine (2015) 'Continuity – textile as silent witness', pp. 44–51 in Jessica Hemmings (ed.) *The Textile Reader*, London and New York: Bloomsbury Academic.

The British Museum (2012) *World Textiles: A Sourcebook*, United Kingdom: British Museum Press.

Broome, André (2009) 'Money for nothing: Everyday actors and monetary crises', *Journal of International Relations and Development*, 12(1): 3–30.

Brown, Chris and Kirsten Ainley (2005) *Understanding International Relations*, 3rd edition, Hampshire and New York: Palgrave Macmillan.

Brown, Hayes (2017) 'The definitive ranking of outfits world leaders have forced each other to wear at APEC', *Buzzfeed News*, https://www.buzzfeednews.com/a rticle/hayesbrown/project-runway-apec-edition

Bryan-Wilson, Julia (2015) 'Lisa Anne Auerbach's canny domesticity', pp. 288–296 in Jessica Hemmings (ed.) *The Textile Reader*, London and New York: Bloomsbury Academic.

Buchli, Victor (2002) 'Introduction', pp. 1–22 in Victor Buchli (ed.) *The Material Culture Reader*, Oxford and New York: Berg.

Buchli, Victor and Gavin Lucas (2001) 'The absent present: Archaeologies of the contemporary past', pp. 3–18 in Victor Buchli and Gavin Lucas (eds) *Archaeologies of the Contemporary Past*, London and New York: Routledge.

Buzan, Barry and George Lawson (2015) *The Global Transformation: History, Modernity and the Making of International Relations*, Cambridge and New York: Cambridge University Press.

Caldwell, Dayna L. (2012) 'The Chilean Arpilleristas: Changing national politics through tapestry work', paper 665, Textile Society of America Symposium Proceedings, http://digitalcommons.unl.edu/cgi/viewcontent.cgi?article=1664 &context=tsaconf

Callahan, William A. (2020) *Sensible Politics: Visualizing International Relations*, New York: Oxford University Press.

Cameron, Lynne (2010) 'What is metaphor and why does it matter?', pp. 3–25 in Lynne Cameron and Robert Maslen (eds) *Metaphor Analysis: Research Practice in Applied Linguistics, Social Sciences and the Humanities*, London and Oakville: Equinox.

Cameron, Lynne and Robert Maslen (2010) 'Preface', pp. vii–viii in Lynne Cameron and Robert Maslen (eds) *Metaphor Analysis: Research Practice in Applied Linguistics, Social Sciences and the Humanities*, London and Oakville: Equinox.

Campbell, David (2007) 'Geopolitics and visuality: Sighting the Darfur conflict', *Political Geography*, 26(4): 357–82.

Campbell, Greg (2002) *Blood Diamonds: Tracing the Deadly Path of the World's Most Precious Stones*, New York: Basic Books.

Carver, Terrell (2010) 'Cinematic ontologies and viewer epistemologies: Knowing international politics as moving images', *Global Society*, 24(3): 421–431.

Cashin, Joan E. (2011) 'Trophies of war: Material culture in the civil war era', *Journal of the Civil War Era*, 1(3): 339–367.

Bibliography 69

Caso, Federica and Caitlin Hamilton (eds) (2015) *Popular Culture and World Politics: Theories, Methodologies, Pedagogies*, Bristol: E-IR Publishing.

Cavarero, Adriana (2000) *Relating Narratives: Storytelling and Selfhood*, translated by Paul A. Kottman, London and New York: Routledge.

Ceramics Now (2019) 'Ehren Tool: Production or destruction / craft and Folk Art Museum, Los Angeles', 8 May 2019, https://www.ceramicsnow.org/2012/05/21/ehren-tool-production-or-destruction-cafam-los-angeles/

Christie, Janet (2013) 'Tapestry of Scotland: The people's creation', *The Scotsman*, 31 August 2013, htp://www.scotsman.com/lifestyle/tapestry-of-scotland-the-people-s-creation-1-3069918

Clare, Claudia (2016) *Subversive Ceramics*, London and New York: Bloomsbury.

Clark, Garth (2017) 'Pen and kiln: A brief overview of modern ceramics and critical writing', pp. 3–9 in Andrew Livingstone and Kevin Petrie (eds) *The Ceramics Reader*, London and New York: Bloomsbury Academic.

Clapton, Will and Laura J. Shepherd (2016) 'Lessons from Westeros: Gender and power in Game of Thrones', *Politics*, 37(1): 5–18.

Clement, Tracey (2019) 'Susan Cohn on the personal and political power of jewellery', *Art Guide*, 3 September 2019, https://artguide.com.au/susan-cohn-on-the-personal-and-political-power-of-jewellery

Cohn, Carol (1987) 'Sex and death in the rational world of defense intellectuals', *Signs*, 12(4): 687–718.

Cohn, Carol (ed.) (2013) *Women and Wars: Contested Histories, Uncertain Futures*, UK and USA: Polity Press.

Cohn, Su san (2014) 'Bernhard Schobinger's "Holiday in Cambodia"', https://artjewelryforum.org/node/5062

Cohn, Su san (2015) 'Su san Cohn Uncommon Moments', *Anna Schwartz Gallery*, https://annaschwartzgallery.com/exhibition/uncommon-moments

Connor, Steven (2000) 'Rough magic: Bags', BBC Radio 3, broadcast 9 January 2000, pp. 346–351 in Ben Highmore (ed.) (2002) *The Everyday Life Reader*, London and New York: Routledge.

Cooper, Emmanuel (2000) *10,000 Years of Pottery*, London: The British Museum Press.

Corkhill, Melissa (2016) 'Use your craft to make a statement', https://thegreenparent.co.uk/articles/read/use-your-craft-to-make-a-statement

Crawford, Matthew B. (2009) *Shop Class as Soulcraft: An Inquiry into the Value of Work*, USA: Penguin Books.

Crawshaw, Steve and John Jackson (2011) S*mall Acts of Resistance*: *How Courage, Tenacity, and Ingenuity Can Change the World*, New York: Union Square Press.

Csikszentmihalyi, Mihaly (1990) *Flow: The Psychology of Optimal Experience*, USA: HarperCollins.

Daley, Kate M. (2013) 'Crafty entanglements: Knitting and hard distinctions in aesthetics and political theory', *Contemporary Aesthetics*, 11, http://quod.lib.umich.edu/c/ca/7523862.0011.024/--crafty-entanglements-knitting-and-hard-distinctions?rgn=main;view=fulltext, Accessed 3 October 2014.

70 Bibliography

Dang, Trung Dinh, Sango Mahanty and Thanh Van Nguyen (2010) 'Vietnam's craft villages and water pollution: A review of previous research', working paper for 'Crafting sustainability: Addressing water pollution from Vietnam's craft villages', Australian National University, https://crawford.anu.edu.au/rmap/pd f/_docs/water_pollution_craft/dang_et_al_2010.pdf

Dauphinee, Elizabeth (2007) 'The politics of the body in pain: Reading the ethics of imagery', *Security Dialogue*, 38(2): 139–155.

Dauphinee, Elizabeth (2013) *The Politics of Exile*, London: Routledge.

Davies, Matt (2016) 'Everyday life as critique: Revisiting the everyday in IPE with Henri Lefebvre and Postcolonialism', *International Political Sociology*, 10(1): 22–38.

de Certeau, Michel (1984) *The Practice of Everyday Life*, translated by Steven Rendall, USA: University of California Press.

Deary, Vincent (2015) *How We Are*, Great Britain: Penguin Books.

Delingpole, James (2014) 'How did Colonel Gaddafi get away with such evil for so long?', *The Spectator*, 8 February 2014, https://www.spectator.co.uk/article/ how-did-colonel-gaddafi-get-away-with-such-evil-for-so-long-

Den Besten, Liesbeth (2011) 'Bernhard Schobinger: Meaning in every material', *Metalsmith*, 36(1): 50–57.

Der Derian, James (2005) 'Imaging terror: Logos, pathos and ethos', *Third World Quarterly*, 26(1): 23–37.

Der Derian, James and Michael J. Shapiro (eds) (1989) *International/Intertextual Relations: Postmodern Readings of World Politics*, New York and Toronto: Lexington Books.

Deetz, James (1977) *In Small Things Forgotten: The Archaeology of Early American Life*, New York: Anchor Books.

Dittmer, Jason (2010) *Popular Culture, Geopolitics, and Identity*, United Kingdom: Rowman and Littlefield.

Dittmer, Jason (2013) *Captain America and the Nationalist Superhero: Metaphors, Narratives and Geopolitics*, Philadelphia: Temple University Press.

Dittmer, Jason (2015) 'On Captain America and 'doing' popular culture in the social sciences', pp. 45–50 in Federica Caso and Caitlin Hamilton (eds) *Popular Culture and World Politics: Theories, Methods, Pedagogies*, Bristol: E-IR Press.

Djindjian, François (2000) 'Artefact analysis', Proceedings of the 28th Computer Applications and Quantitative Methods in Archaeology Conference (CAA), Ljubljana, Slovenia, 18–21 April 2000, https://hsbiblio.uni-tuebingen.de/x mlui/bitstream/handle/10900/61178/07_Djindjian_CAA_2000.pdf?sequence=2 &isAllowed=y

Doty, Roxanne Lynn (1993) 'Foreign policy as social construction: A post-positivist analysis of U.S. counterinsurgency policy in the Philippines', *International Studies Quarterly*, 37(3): 297–320.

Doty, Roxanne Lynn (1996) *Imperial Encounters: The Politics of Representation in North-South Relations*, Minneapolis: University of Minnesota Press.

Doty, Roxanne Lynn (2010) 'Autoethnography – making human connections', *Review of International Studies*, 36(4): 104–1050.

Bibliography 71

Duvall, Raymond and Latha Varadarajan (2003) 'On the practical significance of critical International Relations theory', *Asian Journal of Political Science*, 11(2): 75–88.

Edgar, Ray (2019) 'Asylum-seeker jewellery ban prompts an act of hope and resistance', *The Age*, https://www.theage.com.au/entertainment/art-and-design/asylum-seeker-jewellery-ban-prompts-an-act-of-hope-and-resistance-2019 0726-p52b2y.html

Edkins, Jenny (2013) 'Novel writing in international relations: Openings for a creative practice', *Security Dialogue*, 44(4): 281–297.

Eighmy, Jeffrey L. (1981) 'The use of material culture in diachronic anthropology', pp. 31–50 in Richard A. Gould and Michael B. Schiffer (eds) *Modern Material Culture: The Archaeology of Us*, New York: Academic Press.

Elias, Juanita and Lena Rethel (eds) (2016) *The Everyday Political Economy of Southeast Asia*, UK: Cambridge University Press.

Elshtain, Jean Bethke (1997) *Real Politics: At the Center of Everyday Life*, Baltimore and London: The John Hopkins University Press.

Enloe, Cynthia (1993) *The Morning After: Sexual Politics at the End of the Cold War*, Berkeley: University of California Press.

Enloe, Cynthia (2000 [1989]) *Bananas, Beaches and Bases: Making Feminist Sense of International Politics*, Berkeley: University of California Press.

Enloe, Cynthia (2011) 'The mundane matters', *International Political Sociology*, 5(4): 447–450.

Epstein, Charlotte (2008) *The Power of Words in International Relations: Birth of an Anti-Whaling Discourse*, Cambridge, Massachusetts and London, England: MIT Press.

Erickson, Kirstin C. (2015) 'Spanish colonial embroidery and the inscription of heritage in contemporary Northern New Mexico', *Journal of Folklore Research*, 52(1): 1–37.

Esterly, David (2015 [2013]) *The Lost Carving: A Journey to the Heart of Making*, London: Duckworth Overlook.

Fairs, Marcus (2018) 'Susan Cohn plans performances in response to Denmark's controversial "jewellery law"', *De Zeen*, 6 April 2018, https://www.dezeen.com /2018/04/06/susan-cohn-plans-series-of-performances-in-response-to-denmark -jewellery-law/

Fenn, Mark (2017) *Narrative Jewelry: Tales from the Toolbox*, Atglen, PA: Schiffer Publishing Ltd.

Flock, Elizabeth (2011) 'Gaddafi's female bodyguards say they were raped, abused by the Libyan leader', *The Washington Post*, 29 August 2011, https://www.was hingtonpost.com/blogs/blogpost/post/gaddafis-female-bodyguards-say-they -were-raped-abused-by-the-libyan-leader/2011/08/29/gIQA8TOKnJ_blog.html

Florence, Gene and Cathy Florence (2002) *Florence's Big Book of Salt & Pepper Shakers: Identification & Value Guide*, United States: Collector Books.

Florke, Stan (2014) 'Our global neighbours: Cloth and its meaning', Australian Museum, 13 November 2014, http://australianmuseum.net.au/blogpost/science /our-global-neighbours-cloth-and-its-meaning

72 Bibliography

Franklin, M.I. (ed.) (2005) *Resounding International Relations: On Music, Culture, and Politics*, London: Palgrave Macmillan.

Fredericks, Bronwyn, Karen Adams, Summer Finlay, Gillian Fletcher, Simone Andy, Lyn Briggs, Lisa Briggs and Robert Hall (2011) 'Engaging the practice of yarning in Action Research', *ALAR Journal*, 17(2): 7–19.

Gardiner, Michael (2000) *Critiques of Everyday Life: An Introduction*, London and New York: Routledge.

Gaver, Bill, Tony Dunne and Alena Pacenti (1999) 'Design: Cultural probes', *Interactions*, 6(1): 21–29.

Geia, Lynore K., Barbara Hayes and Kim Usher (2013) 'Yarning/Aboriginal storytelling: Towards an understanding of an Indigenous perspective and its implications for research practice', *Contemporary Nurse*, 46(1): 13–17.

George, William Lloyd (2010) 'Hmong refugees live in fear in Laos and Thailand', *Time*, 24 July 2010, http://content.time.com/time/world/article/0,8599,2005706,00.html

Gero, Annette (2015) *Wartime Quilts: Appliqués and Geometric Masterpieces from Military Fabrics*, NSW, Australia: The Beagle Press.

Gianturco, Paola and Toby Tuttle (2004) *In Her Hands*, 2nd edition, Brooklyn: Powerhouse Books.

Gilbert, Elizabeth (2015) *Big Magic*, Great Britain: Bloomsbury Publishing.

Ginsborg, Paul (2005) *The Politics of Everyday Life: Making Choices, Changing Lives*, New Haven and London: Yale University Press.

Gómez, Sarahmaria (2011) 'The art of Colcha embroidery', *YouTube*, 9 October 2011, https://www.youtube.com/watch?v=FII7LUpwXqk

Goodman, Nelson (1985) 'How buildings mean', *Critical Inquiry*, 11(4): 642–653.

Goodsell, Charles T. (1988) 'The architecture of parliaments: Legislative houses and political culture', *British Journal of Political Science*, 18(3): 287–302.

Gordon, Beverly (2013) *Textiles: The Whole Story – Uses, Meaning, Significance*, United Kingdom: Thames & Hudson.

Gottschall, Jonathan (2013) *The Storytellling Animal: How Stories Make Us Human*, USA: Houghton Mifflin Harcourt.

Gould, Richard A. and Michael B. Schiffer (eds) *Modern Material Culture: The Archaeology of Us*, New York: Academic Press.

Gowan, Richard (2014) 'Failed peacemaking efforts make 2014 year of dead-end diplomacy', *World Politics Review*, 8 December 2014, http://www.worldpoliticsreview.com/articles/14601/failed-peacemaking-efforts-make-2014-year-of-dead-end-diplomacy

Goyanes, Rob (2017) 'This artist is making ceramics to honor people of color, from Obama to Biggie', 15 May 2017, https://www.artsy.net/article/artsy-editorial-artist-making-ceramics-honor-people-color-obama-biggie

Gray, M. David (2003) 'Thread and wool tradition', *The Santa Fe New Mexican*, 14 July 2013, http://tumultimedia.org/colcha/Thread_Wool_Tradition.html

Grayson, Kyle, Matt Davies and Simon Philpott (2009), 'Pop goes IR? Researching the popular culture-world politics continuum', *Politics*, 29(3): 155–163.

Bibliography 73

The Great Tapestry of Scotland (n.d.) 'Panels and those who stitched them', http://scotlandstapestry.com/index.php?s=tapestry

Green, Laura Marcus (2012) 'New Mexico Colcha Club: Spanish colonial embroidery and the women who saved it [book review]', *Journal of American Folklore*, 125(495): 126–134.

Greene, Alan F. (2012) 'Where pottery and politics meet: Mundane objects and complex political life in the late Bronze Age South Caucasus', pp. 302–322 in Charles W. Hartley, G. Bike Yazicioğlu and Adam T. Smith (eds) *The Archaeology of Power and Politics in Eurasia*, London: Cambridge University Press.

Greenhalgh, Paul (2017) 'Social complexity and the historiography of ceramic', pp. 258–262 in Andrew Livingstone and Kevin Petrie (eds) (2017) *The Ceramics Reader*, London and New York: Bloomsbury Academic.

Griffin, Penny (2015) *Political Culture, Political Economy and the Death of Feminism: Why Women Are in Refrigerators and Other Stories*, Oxon and New York: Routledge.

Gualberti, Stefania (2015) 'Arpillera journeys', *Innate*, http://www.innatenonviolence.org/readings/2015_06.shtml

Guillaume, Xavier (2011) 'The international as an everyday practice', *International Political Sociology*, 5(4): 446–462.

Guillaume, Xavier and Jef Huysmans (2019) 'The concept of "the everyday": Ephemeral politics and the abundance of life', *Cooperation and Conflict*, 54(2): 278–296.

Hagström and Gastafsson (2019) 'Narrative power: How storytelling shapes East Asian international politics', *Cambridge Review of International Affairs*, 32(4): 387–406.

Hamilton, Caitlin (2019) 'Exploring the potential of the popular culture and world politics agenda: Actors, artefacts and the everyday', *Australian Journal of Political Science*, 54(4): 573–584.

Hamilton, Caitlin and Laura J. Shepherd (eds) (2016) *Understanding Popular Culture and World Politics in the Digital Age*, London and New York: Routledge.

Hamilton, David (1974) *Manual of Pottery and Ceramics*, London: Thames and Hudson.

Hansen, Lene (2006) *Security as Practice: Discourse Analysis and the Bosnian War*, Oxon and New York: Routledge.

Hashimoto, Kyoko (n.d.) 'Coal necklace', https://www.kyokohashimoto.com/works#/coal-necklace/

Haynes, Jeffrey, Peter Hough, Shahin Malik and Lloyd Pettiford (2011) *World Politics*, England: Pearson.

Heart Roots Art (n.d.) 'American/Soviet Clay Stomp June 11, 1989 Milwaukee, Wisconsin', https://www.heartrootsart.com/past-projects?lightbox=dataItem-k7hvs6sr3

Heller, Ágnes (1984) *Everyday Life*, translated by G.L. Campbell, London, Boston, Melbourne and Henley: Routledge and Kegan Paul.

Hemmings, Jessica (ed.) (2015) *The Textile Reader*, London, New Delhi, New York and Sydney: Bloomsbury.

74 Bibliography

Herbert, Lisa (2020) 'Sculptors and ceramicists donate works to raise fire recovery funds', *About Regional*, https://aboutregional.com.au/sculptors-and-ceramicists-donate-works-to-raise-fire-recovery-funds/

Hermann, Tove (2012) 'Knitting as Dissent: Female resistance in America since the revolutionary war', *Textile Society of America Symposium Proceedings*, http://digitalcommons.unl.edu/cgi/viewcontent.cgi?article=1695&context=tsaconf

Heywood, Andrew (2011) *Global Politics*, UK and US: Palgrave Macmillan.

Highmore, Ben (2002) *Everyday Life and Cultural Theory: An Introduction*, London and New York: Routledge.

Hobbes, Thomas (1651) *Leviathan*, http://glücksmann.de/media/files/Hobbes-Leviathan.pdf

Hobson, John M. and Leonard Seabrooke (eds) (2007) *Everyday Politics of the World Economy*, New York: Cambridge University Press.

Hodder, Ian (2003) 'The interpretation of documents and material culture', pp. 155–175 in Norman K. Denzin and Yvonna S. Lincoln (eds) *Collecting and Interpreting Qualitative Materials*, Thousand Oaks, London and New Delhi: SAGE Publications.

Hoskins, Janet (2006) 'Agency, biography and objects', pp. 74–84 in Chris Tilley, Well Keane, Susanne Küchler, Mike Rowlands and Patricia Spyer (eds) *Handbook of Material Culture*, London, Thousand Oaks, New Delhi: SAGE Publications.

Hoskyns, Catherine and Shirin M. Rai (2007) 'Recasting the global political economy: Counting women's unpaid work', *New Political Economy*, 12(3): 297–317.

Howes, David (2006) 'Scent, sound and synaesthesia: Intersensoriality and Material Culture Theory', pp. 161–172 in Chris Tilley, Webb Keane, Susanne Küchler, Mike Rowlands and Patricia Spyer (eds) *Handbook of Material Culture*, London, Thousand Oaks, New Delhi: SAGE Publications.

Hozić, Aida A. (2017) 'Introduction: The aesthetic turn at 15 (legacies, limits and prospects)', *Millennium: Journal of International Studies*, 45(2): 201–205.

Human Rights Watch (2020) 'Emergency action needed for vulnerable artisanal and small-scale mining communities and supply chains', https://www.hrw.org/news/2020/05/13/emergency-action-needed-vulnerable-artisanal-small-scale-mining-communities-supply

Hunt, Barb (n.d.) 'Antipersonnel', https://barbhuntca.wordpress.com/2021/01/14/antipersonnel/

Hyman, N. Richard (1953) *Ceramics Handbook*, New York: ARCO Publishing Company.

Inayatullah, Naeem (ed.) (2010) *Autobiographical International Relations: I, IR*, New York: Routledge.

Inayatullah, Naeem and Elizabeth Dauphinee (2017) *Narrative Global Politics: Theory, History and the Personal in International Relations*, London: Routledge.

Jackson, Patrick Thaddeus (2015) 'Must international studies be a science?', *Millennium: Journal of International Studies*, 43(3): 942–965.

Bibliography 75

Jacobsen, Michael Hviid (2009) 'Introduction: The everyday: An introduction to an introduction', pp. 1–42 in Michael Hviid Jacobsen (ed.) *Encountering the Everyday: An Introduction to the Sociologies of the Unnoticed*, Basingstoke and New York: Palgrave MacMillan.

Jao, Carren (2012) 'The cups of war', *Hyperallergic*, 18 June 2012, hyperallergic .com/53007/the-cups-of-war/

Johnson, Rachel and Shirin M. Rai (2012) 'Imagining pasts and futures: The Indian Parliament Murals and South Africa's Keiskamma Tapestry', *openIndia*, 14 December 2012, www.opendemocracy.net/openindia/rachel-johnson-shirin -m-rai/imagining-pasts-and-futures-indian-parliament-murals-and-south

Jolly, Lucinda (2014) 'Now we reap the wonder they sew with Keiskamma Tapestry', *Mail and Guardian*, 10 January 2014, mg.co.za/article/2014-01-09 -now-we-reap-the-wonder-they-sew

Jones, Dorothy (2003) 'Embroidering the nation', *Textile: The Journal of Cloth and Culture*, 1(2): 174–193.

Jørgensen, Marianne (2006) 'Pink M.24 Chaffee: A tank wrapped in pink', web .archive.org/web/20061129212235/http://www.marianneart.dk/

Juneau, Thomas and Mira Sucharov (2010) 'Narratives in pencil: Using graphic novels to teach Israeli-Palestinian relations', *International Studies Perspectives*, 11(2): 172–183.

Kaplan, Alice and Kristin Ross (1987) 'Introduction', *Yale French Studies*, 73: 1–4.

Kelly, Tara (2011) 'Tony Casdagli, British POW's son, shares encrypted cross-stitching tale', *The Huffington Post*, 9 September 2011, www.huffingtonpost.c om/2011/09/09/cross-stitching-world-war-ii_n_955167.html

Keohane, Robert O. (1988) 'International institutions: Two approaches', *International Studies Quarterly*, 32(4): 379–396.

Kerkvliet, Benedict J. (2005) *The Power of Everyday Politics: How Vietnamese Peasants Transformed National Policy*, USA: Cornell University Press.

Kingery, W. David (1996) 'Introduction', pp. 1–15 in David W. Kingery (ed.) *Learning from Things: Method and Theory of Material Culture Studies*, Washington and London: Smithsonian Institution Press.

Kirsehnblatt-Gimblett, Barbara (2005) 'Ties that bind: A conversation about heritage, authenticity, and war textiles', pp. 47–55 in Ariel Zeitlin Cooke and Marsha MacDowell (eds) *Weavings of War: Fabrics of Memory*, USA: Michigan State University Museum.

Kirwan, Padraig (2016) 'Choctaw Tales: An interview with LeAnne Howe', *Women: A Cultural Review*, 27(3): 265–279.

Knowles, Elizabeth M. (1999) *The Oxford Dictionary of Quotations*, Oxford: Oxford University Press.

Koobak, Redi (2014) 'Writing in stuck places', pp. 194–207 in Lykke, Nina (ed.) *Writing Academic Texts Differently: Intersectional Feminist Methodologies and the Playful Art of Writing*, New York and London: Routledge.

Korn, Peter (2017 [2013]) *Why We Make Things & Why It Matters: The Education of a Craftsman*, London: Vintage.

76   Bibliography

Kuusisto, Rikka (2019) *International Relations Narratives: Plotting World Politics*, London: Routledge.

Kuzma, Lynn M. and Patrick J. Haney (2001) 'And... action! Using film to learn about foreign policy', *International Studies Perspectives*, 2(1): 33–50.

Laarhoven, Ruurdje (2012) 'Textile trade war: Batik revival as political weapon in 17th century Java', *Textile Society of America Symposium Proceedings*, http://digitalcommons.unl.edu/cgi/viewcontent.cgi?article=1704&context=tsaconf

Lahiri-Dutt, Kuntala and Gill Burke (2011) 'Gender mainstreaming in Asian mining: A development perspective', pp. 213–230 in Kuntala Lahiri-Dutt (ed.) *Gendering the Field: Towards Sustainable Livelihoods for Mining Communities*, Australia: ANU Press.

Lakoff, George (1991) 'Metaphors and war: The metaphor system used to justify war in the Gulf', paper presented at Alumni House, University of California at Berkeley, 30 January 1991, eprints.cdlib.org/uc/item/9sm131vj#page-1

Lakoff, George and Johnson, Mark (1980) *Metaphors We Live By*, Chicago and London, The University of Chicago Press.

Langley, Paul (2008) *The Everyday Life of Global Finance: Saving and Borrowing in Anglo-America*, Oxford and New York: Oxford University Press.

Lantern (2019) 'Building community from clay', 1 August 2019, lantern.uwlax.edu /building-community-from-clay

Laurenson, Sarah (2018) 'Collecting the present: A tea set that helps us rethink the past', *National Museums Scotland*, https://blog.nms.ac.uk/2018/11/13/collec ting-the-present-a-tea-set-that-helps-us-rethink-the-past/

Law, John (2004) *After Method: Mess in Social Science Research*, London and New York: Routledge.

Leach, Bernard (2011) *A Potter's Book*, London: Faber and Faber.

Lefebvre, Henri (1991 [1958]) *Critique of Everyday Life*, Volume 1, translated by John Moore, London and New York: Verso.

Lefebvre, Henri (1987) 'The everyday and everydayness', translated by Christine Levich, *Yale French Studies*, 73: 7–11.

Leggo, Carl (2008) 'Narrative inquiry: Attending to the art of discourse', *Language and Literacy*, 10(1), www.langandlit.ualberta.ca/current.html

Lilja, Mona and Stellan Vinthagen (2018) 'Dispersed resistance: Unpacking the spectrum and properties of glaring and everyday resistance', *Journal of Political Power*, 11(2): 211–229.

Ling, L.H.M. (2014) *The Dao of World Politics: Towards a Post-Westphalian, Worldist International Relations*, Oxon and New York: Routledge.

Lipson, Elaine (2012) 'The slow cloth manifesto: An alternative to the politics of production', Paper presented at the Textile Society of America Symposium Proceedings, paper 711, https://digitalcommons.unl.edu/tsaconf/711/

Lor, Xai S. (n.d.) 'Acknowledgement for the www.HmongEmbroidery.org Project and a brief history of Paj Ntaub', HmongEmbroidery.org, http://www .hmongembroidery.org

Lothian, Sayraphim (2014) 'Week #3 of 48 weeks of historical craftivism, Greenham Common Women's Peace Camp', *Craftivism*, 22 February 2014, www.crafti

Bibliography 77

vism.com/blog/week-3-of-48-weeks-of-historical-craftivism-greenham-com mon-womens-peace-camp/

Lüdtke, Alf (ed.) (1995) *The History of Everyday Life: Reconstructing Historical Experiences and Ways of Life*, translated by William Templer, New Jersey: Princeton University Press.

Lugo, Robert (2020) 'Press release: *To Disarm*', *Artsy*, www.artsy.net/show/wexler -gallery-to-disarm-new-work-by-roberto-lugo

Mac Ginty, Roger (2014) 'Everyday peace: Bottom-up and local agency in conflict-affected societies', *Security Dialogue*, 45(6): 548–564.

Mac Ginty, Roger (2019) 'Circuits, the everyday and international relations: Connecting the home to the international and transnational', *Cooperation and Conflict*, 54(2): 234–253.

MacAulay, Suzanne Pollock (2000) *Stitching Rites: Colcha Embroidery Along the Northern Rio Grande*, Tucson: University of Arizona Press.

MacAulay, Suzanne P. (2010) 'Colcha embroidery as cartography: Mapping landscapes of memory and passage', Textile Society of America Symposium Proceedings, https://digitalcommons.unl.edu/tsaconf/36/

MacGregor, Neil (2012) *A History of the World in 100 Objects*, Great Britain: Penguin Books.

Macwhirter, Iain (2007) 'Burns benighted', *The Guardian*, 26 January 2007, www.t heguardian.com/commentisfree/2007/jan/25/burnswould probablyhavebeen

Malecka, Anna (2018) 'Koh-i Noor diamond and Babur's Stone: Issue of identity', *Iran*, 58(1): 84–92.

Manchester Art Gallery (2014) 'Bernhard Schobinger: The rings of Saturn', www. manchesterartgallery.org/exhibitions-and-events/exhibition/bernhard-schobin ger-the-rings-of-saturn/

Mannergren Selimovic, Johanna (2019) 'Everyday agency and transformation: Place, body and story in the divided city', *Cooperation and Conflict*, 54(2): 131–148.

Mansbach, Richard W. and Kirsten L. Taylor (2012) *Introduction to Global Politics*, 2nd edition, Oxon and New York: Routledge.

Mascelloni, Enrico (2009) *War Rugs: The Nightmare of Modernism*, translated by Rosa Maria Falvo, Milan: Skira.

Mathieu Paul (1999/2000a) *Shoah, 33–45*, http://www.paulmathieu.ca/?p=3291

Mathieu Paul (1999/2000b) *Dallas 63*, http://www.paulmathieu.ca/?p=3298

Mathieu Paul (1999/2000c) *Oklahoma City 95*, http://www.paulmathieu.ca/?p=3304

Mathieu Paul (1999/2000d) *Oka Crisis 90*, http://www.paulmathieu.ca/?p=3349

Mathieu Paul (1999/2000e) *Hiroshima 45*, http://www.paulmathieu.ca/?p=3354

Mathieu Paul (2000) *Disasters*, http://www.paulmathieu.ca/?p=3762

Mathieu Paul (2002) *W.T.C. 9–11, 2001*, http://www.paulmathieu.ca/?p=3282

Mattingly, Cheryl, Mary Lawlor and Lanita Jacobs-Huey (2002) 'Narrating September 11: Race, gender, and the play of cultural identities', *American Anthropologist*, 104(3): 743–753.

McCracken, Sarah (2011) 'Arpilleras: A visual history of the poor under Pinochet', *Prospect Journal of International Affairs at UCSD*, 24 August 2011, http://pro

78   *Bibliography*

spectjournal.org/2011/08/24/arpilleras-a-visual-history-of-the-poor-under-p inochet/

McCullough, D.M. (2014) 'Deforestation for fashion: Getting unsustainable fabrics out of the closet', *The Guardian*, 25 April 2014, http://www.theguardian.com/sus tainable-business/zara-h-m-fashion-sustainable-forests-logging-fabric

McDougall, Ruth (2011) 'Maps of history: Hmong pha pra vet (storytelling) cloths', pp. 62–68 in Queensland Art Gallery, *Gallery of Modern Art, Threads: Contemporary Textiles and the Social Fabric*, Queensland: Queensland Art Gallery, Gallery of Modern Art.

McElroy, Gil (2015) 'Barb Hunt: Antipersonnel', International Sculpture Center, 28 January 2015, blog.sculpture.org/2015/01/28/barb-hunt-antipersonnel/

Médecins Sans Frontières (2008) 'Thailand forcibly returns hundreds of Hmong refugees to Laos', 25 June 2008, http://www.doctorswithoutborders.org/news -stories/press-release/thailand-forcibly-returns-hundreds-hmong-refugees-laos

The Metropolitan Museum of Art (2014) 'Conquest, conflict, and the global textile trade', www.metmuseum.org/exhibitions/listings/2013/interwoven-globe/conq uest-conflict

Migdal, Joel S. (2013) 'Foreword', in Adam White (ed.) *The Everyday Life of the State*, pp. vii–xiv, Seattle: Center for Global Studies, Jackson School of International Studies in Association with University of Washington Press.

Milliken, Jennifer (1999) 'The study of discourse in International Relations: A critique of research methods', *European Journal of International Relations*, 5(2): 225–254.

Minh-ha, Trinh T. (1989) *Woman, Native, Other: Writing Postcoloniality and Feminism*, Bloomington and Indianapolis: Indiana University Press.

Mitchell, W.J.T. (1986) *Iconology: Image, Text, Ideology*, Chicago and London: The University of Chicago Press.

Möller, Frank (2013) *Visual Peace: Images, Spectatorship, and the Politics of Violence*, United Kingdom: Palgrave Macmillan.

Moran, Joe (2005) *Reading the Everyday*, Oxon and New York: Routledge.

Moran, Joe (2007) *Queuing for Beginners: The Story of Daily Life from Breakfast to Bedtime*, Great Britain: Profile Books.

Moreland, John (2001) *Archaeology and Text*, London: Gerald Duckworth & Co.

Mould, Tom (2003) *Choctaw Prophecy: A Legacy for the Future*, USA: University of Alabama Press.

Mould, Tom (2004) *Choctaw Tales*, Jackson: University Press of Mississippi.

Mukherjee, Swapna (2013) *The Science of Clays*, Dordrecht: Springer.

Mydans, Seth (2009) 'Thailand begins repatriation of Hmong to Laos', *The New York Times*, 27 December 2009, http://www.nytimes.com/2009/12/28/world/ asia/28hmong.html?_r=0

Naumes, Sarah (2015) 'Is all "I" IR?', *Millennium: Journal of International Studies*, 43(3): 820–832.

Nelson, Kathryn J. (1980) 'Excerpts from "Los Testamentos": Hispanic women folk artists of the San Luis Valley, Colorado', *Frontiers: A Journal of Women Studies*, 5(3): 34–43.

Bibliography 79

Newell, Stephanie (2006) *West African Literatures: Ways of Reading*, Oxford: Oxford University Press.

Nieder, Alison A. (2015) 'California needs its own fabric', *California Apparel News*, 19 January 2015, https://www.apparelnews.net/news/2015/jan/19/california-needs-its-own-fabric/

Norum, Karen E. (2008) 'Artifacts', in Lisa M. Given (ed.) *The Sage Encyclopedia of Qualitative Research Methods*, https://dx.doi.org/10.4135/9781412963909

Olsen, Bjørnar Julius (2006) 'Scenes from a troubled engagement: Post-structuralism and material culture studies', pp. 85–103 in Chris Tilley, Webb Keane, Susanne Küchler, Mike Rowlands and Patricia Spyer (eds) *Handbook of Material Culture*, London, Thousand Oaks, New Delhi: SAGE Publications.

Ostermann, Matthias (2006) *The Ceramic Narrative*, London: A & C Black, and Philadelphia: University of Pennsylvania Press.

Ouattara, Issiaka (2018) 'The Griots of West Africa: Oral tradition and ancestral knowledge', translated by Charity Fox, pp. 151–167 in Bernd Reiter (ed.) *Constructing the Pluriverse*, USA: Duke University Press.

Parker, Rozsika (1984) *The Subversive Stitch*, Great Britain: The Women's Press.

Parkinson, John R. (2012) *Democracy and Public Space: The Physical Sites of Democratic Performance*, Oxford: Oxford University Press.

The Parliament House Embroidery Committee (1988) *A Work of Many Hands*, Canberra: Australian Government Publishing Service.

Parliament of the Republic of South Africa (n.d.) 'Parliamentary art', https://www.parliament.gov.za/parliamentary-art.

Pearce, Susan M. (1994a) 'Museum objects', pp. 9–11 in Susan M. Pearce (ed.) *Interpreting Objects and Collections*, London: Routledge.

Pearce, Susan M. (1994b) 'Thinking about things', pp. 125–132 in Susan M. Pearce (ed.) *Interpreting Objects and Collections*, London: Routledge.

Perec, Georges (1997) *Species of Spaces and Other Pieces*, edited and translated by John Sturrock, London: Penguin Books.

Phillips, Clare (1996) *Jewelry: From Antiquity to the Present*, UK: Thames & Hudson.

Popovic and Miller (2015) *Blueprint for Revolution: How to Use Rice Pudding, Lego Men, and Other Nonviolent Techniques to Galvanize Communities, Overthrow Dictators, or Simply Change the World*, New York: Random House.

Poushter, Jacob (2016) 'Smartphone ownership and internet usage continues to climb in emerging economies', Pew Research Centre, https://www.pewresearch.org/global/2016/02/22/smartphone-ownership-and-internet-usage-continues-to-climb-in-emerging-economies/

Potters for Peace/Ceramistas por la Paz (n.d.) 'About potters for peace', https://www.pottersforpeace.org/about-us.

Potters without Borders (n.d.) 'About us', www.potterswithoutborders.com/aboutus-2/

Powell, Nate (2019) 'About face', *Popula*, 24 February 2019, https://popula.com/2019/02/24/about-face/

80 Bibliography

Prain, Leanne (2014) *Strange Material: Storytelling Through Textiles*, Vancouver: Arsenal Pulp Press.

Prown, Jules (1994) 'Mind in matter: An introduction to material culture theory and method', pp. 133–138 in Susan M. Pearce (ed.) *Interpreting Objects and Collections*, London: Routledge.

Pruitt, Lesley (2013) *Youth Peacebuilding: Music, Gender, and Change*, New York: SUNY Press.

Raden, Aja (2016) *Stoned*, New York: Ecco.

Rai, Shirin M. (2010) 'Analysing ceremony and ritual in parliament', *The Journal of Legislative Studies*, 16(3): 284–297.

Rainforth, Dylan (2015) 'Jeweller Susan Cohn creates golden toe tag for friend to be buried with', *The Sydney Morning Herald*, 25 August 2015, https://www.smh.com.au/entertainment/art-and-design/jeweller-susan-cohn-creates-golden-toe-tag-for-friend-to-be-buried-with-20150825-gj6yem.html

Ramachandra, Komala (2020) 'Forced labor persists in Uzbekistan's cotton fields', Human Rights Watch, https://www.hrw.org/news/2020/06/25/forced-labor-persists-uzbekistans-cotton-fields

Rawson, Philip (1971) *Ceramics*, London: Oxford University Press.

Rice, Prudence M. (2005 [1987]) *Pottery Analysis: A Sourcebook*, Chicago and London: The University of Chicago Press.

Roberts, Kathaleen (2014) 'Colcha embroidery exhibit in Española', Venue, 3 August 2014, http://www.abqjournal.com/439950/entertainment/colcha-embroidery-exhibit-in-espantildeola.html

Rodriguez, Deborah (2014) *The House on Carnaval Street: A Memoir*, New South Wales: Random House Australia.

Rose, Gillian (2001) *Visual Methodologies: An Introduction to the Interpretation of Visual Materials*, London, Thousand Oaks and New Delhi: SAGE Publications.

Rowlands, Michael and Christopher Tilley (2006) 'Monuments and memorials', pp. 500–515 in Chris Tilley, Webb Keane, Susanne Küchler, Mike Rowlands and Patricia Spyer (eds) *Handbook of Material Culture*, London, Thousand Oaks, New Delhi: SAGE Publications.

Rowley, Christina (2015 [2010]) 'Popular culture and the politics of the visual', pp. 309–325 in Laura J. Shepherd (ed.) *Gender Matters in Global Politics: A Feminist Introduction to International Relations*, New York and London: Routledge.

Rowley, Christina and Jutta Weldes (2012) 'The evolution of international security studies and the everyday: Suggestions from the Buffyverse', *Security Dialogue*, 43(6): 513–530.

Russell, Kate and Barnett, Pennina (1987) 'Craft as art', pp. 65–73 in Gillian Elinor, Su Richardson, Sue Scott, Angharad Thomas and Kate Walker (eds) *Women and Craft: Domestic Craftwork*, Great Britain: Virago.

Salter, Mark B. (ed.) (2015) *Making Things International 1: Circuits and Motion*, Minneapolis and London: University of Minnesota Press.

Salter, Mark B. (2015) 'Introduction', pp. vii–xxii in Mark Salter (ed.) *Making Things International 1: Circuits and Motion*, Minneapolis and London: University of Minnesota Press.

Bibliography 81

Saracino, Stephen (1984) 'Third world civilian ring', https://stephensaracino.com/2020/01/02/third-world-civilian-ring/

Saracino, Stephen (1993) 'Green Line Sedan', https://stephensaracino.com/2019/07/31/green-line-sedan/

Saracino, Stephen (1995) 'Lockerbie Flight Bracelet', https://stephensaracino.com/2020/01/02/lockerbie-flight-bracelet/

Särmä, Saara (2012) 'Gendered parodies of nuclear Iran', pp. 151–170 in Pami Aalto, Vilho Harle and Sami Moisio (eds) *Global and Regional Problems: Towards an Interdisciplinary Study*, Surrey: Ashgate Publishing Limited.

Särmä, Saara (2014) *Junk Feminism and Nuclear Wannabes - Collaging Parodies of Iran and North Korea*, Tampere: Tampere University Press.

Särmä, Saara (2015) 'Collage: An art-inspired methodology for studying laughter in world politics', pp. 110–119 in Federica Caso and Caitlin Hamilton (eds) *Popular Culture and World Politics: Theories, Methods, Pedagogies*, Bristol: E-IR Publishing.

Särmä, Saara (2016) 'Collaging internet parody images: An art-inspired methodology for studying laughter in world politics', pp. 175–188 in Caitlin Hamilton and Laura Shepherd (eds) *Understanding World Politics and Popular Culture in the Digital Age*, London and New York: Routledge.

Saunders, Nicholas J. (2002) 'Memory and conflict', pp. 175–180 in Victor Buchli (ed.) *The Material Culture Reader*, Oxford and New York: Berg.

Scheid, Dwayne (2015) 'The political economy of ceramic production in Barbados: From plantation industry to craft production', PhD dissertation, https://surface.syr.edu/cgi/viewcontent.cgi?article=1329&context=etd

Schiffer, Michael Brian (1999) *Material Life of Human Beings: Artifacts, Behavior and Communication*, London: Routledge.

Schmahmann, Brenda (2011) 'After Bayeux: The Keiskamma Tapestry and the making of South African history', *Textile: The Journal of Cloth and Culture*, 9(2): 158–193.

Schulz, Vera-Simone (2014) 'Portraits, photographs, and politics in the carpet medium: Iran, the Soviet Union and beyond', *Konsthistorisk tidskrift / Journal of Art History*, 83(3): 244–265.

The Scottish Parliament (2013) 'One of the world's longest tapestries is unveiled at the Scottish Parliament', http://www.scottish.parliament.uk/newsandmediacentre/66777.aspx

Shapiro, Michael J. (2009) *Cinematic Geopolitics*, London and New York: Routledge.

Shelton, Anthony Alan (2006) 'Museums and museum displays', pp. 480–499 in Chris Tilley, Webb Keane, Susanne Küchler, Mike Rowlands and Patricia Spyer (eds) *Handbook of Material Culture*, London, Thousand Oaks, New Delhi: SAGE Publications.

Shepherd, Laura J. (2013a) *Telling Stories: Gender, Violence and Popular Culture*, Oxon and New York: Routledge.

Shepherd, Laura J. (2013b) 'Introduction: Critical approaches to security in contemporary global politics', pp. 1–8 in Laura J. Shepherd (ed.) *Critical*

82 Bibliography

Approaches to Security: An Introduction to Theories and Methods, London and New York: Routledge.

Shepherd, Laura J. (2018) 'Militarisation', pp. 209–214 in Roland Bleiker (ed.) *Visual Global Politics*, London: Routledge.

Shepherd, Laura J. (2021) *Narrating the Women, Peace and Security Agenda: Logics of Global Governance*, New York: Oxford University Press.

Sheringham, Michael (2006) *Everyday Life: Theories and Practices from Surrealism to the Present*, New York: Oxford University Press.

Sirch, Willow Ann (2015) 'Arpilleras', *The Unfinished Quilter*, http://www.unfinishedquilter.com/arpilleras.html

Sherwell (1996) 'Palestinian costume, the Intifada and the gendering of nationalist discourse', *Journal of Gender Studies*, 5(3): 293–303.

Skibo, James M. (1994) 'Pottery and people', pp. 1–8 in James Skibo and Gary Feinman (eds) *Pottery and People: A Dynamic Interaction*, USA: University of Utah Press.

Smith, Dorothy E. (1987) *Everyday World as Problematic: A Feminist Sociology*, Boston: Northeastern University Press.

Smith, Steve (2004) 'Singing our world into existence: International Relations theory and September 11', *International Studies Quarterly*, 48(3): 499–515.

Snook, Margaret (2010) 'Chilean arpilleras: A chapter of history written on cloth', Cachando Chile: Reflections on Chilean Culture, 11 September 2010, https://cachandochile.wordpress.com/2010/09/11/chilean-arpilleras-a-chapter-of-history-written-on-cloth/

Sonter, Laura J., Diego Herrera, Damian J. Barrett, Gillian L. Galford, Chris J. Moran, and Britaldo S. Soareas-Filho (2017) 'Mining drives extensive deforestation in the Brazilian Amazon', *Nature Communications*, 8(1013).

Spencer, Richard (2011) 'Colonel Gaddafi: And to think we once found this ferocious tyrant funny', *The Telegraph*, https://www.telegraph.co.uk/news/worldnews/africaandindianocean/libya/8803153/Colonel-Gaddafi-And-to-think-we-once-found-this-ferocious-tyrant-funny.html

Spiegelman, Art (2003) *The Complete Maus*, UK: Penguin.

Stahl, Roger (2006) 'Have you played the War on Terror?', *Critical Studies in Media Communication*, 23(2): 112–230.

Stewart, Susan (2003) *On Longing: Narratives of the Miniature, the Gigantic, the Souvenir, the Collection*, USA: Duke University Press.

Stiles, Kaelyn, Özlem Altıok and Michael M. Bell (2011) 'The ghosts of taste: Food and the cultural politics of authenticity', *Agriculture and Human Values*, 28(2): 225–236.

Sudjic, Deyan (2011 [2005]) *The Edifice Complex: The Architecture of Power*, England: Penguin Books.

Suganami, Hidemi (2008) 'Narrative explanation and international relations: Back to basics', *Millennium: Journal of International Studies*, 37(2): 327–356.

Sylvester, Christine (2001) 'Art, abstraction, and international relations', *Millennium: Journal of International Studies*, 30(3): 535–554.

Sylvester, Christine (2009) *Art/Museums: International Relations Where We Least Expect It*, Boulder: Paradigm Publishers.

Bibliography 83

Sylvester, Christine (2013a) 'Experiencing the end and afterlives of International Relations/theory', *European Journal of International Relations*, 19(3): 609–626.

Sylvester, Christine (2013b) *War as Experience*, Oxon and New York: Routledge.

Tapply, Sue (2013) 'Seven miles of pink wool for peace', http://www.womensviewsonnews.org/2013/11/seven-miles-of-pink-wool-for-peace/

Tétreault, Mary Ann and Lipschutz, Ronnie D. (2009) *Global Politics as if People Mattered*, 2nd edition, USA: Rowman and Littlefield Publishers.

Texas State Library and Archives Commission (n.d.) 'Texas state symbols', https://www.tsl.texas.gov/ref/abouttx/symbols.html

Tickner, Arlene B. (2013) 'By way of conclusion?: Forget IR?', pp. 214–232 in Arlene B. Tickner, Arlene B. and David L. Blaney (eds) *Claiming the International*, London and New York: Routledge.

Tickner, J. Ann (2001) *Gendering World Politics: Issues and Approaches in the Post-Cold War Era*, USA: Columbia University Press.

Tidy, Joanna (2019) 'War craft: The embodied politics of making war', *Security Dialogue*, 50(3): 220–238.

Tilley, Christopher (1994) 'Interpreting material culture', 67–75 in Susan M. Pearce (ed.) *Interpreting Objects and Collections*, London and New York: Routledge.

Tilley, Christopher (2002) 'Metaphor, materiality and interpretation', pp. 23–26 in Victor Buchli (ed.) *The Material Culture Reader*, Oxford and New York: Berg.

Tilley, Chris, Well Keane, Susanne Küchler, Mike Rowlands and Patricia Spyer (2006) 'Introduction', pp. 1–6 in Chris Tilley, Webb Keane, Susanne Küchler, Mike Rowlands and Patricia Spyer (eds) *Handbook of Material Culture*, London, Thousand Oaks, New Delhi: SAGE Publications.

Tipton, Barbara (1990) *Answers to Potters Questions: Selected form the Ceramics Monthly Questions Column*, Ohio: Professional Publications, Inc.

Tool, Ehren (2018) 'I just make cups', https://studiopotter.org/i-just-make-cups-0

Tool, Ehren (n.d.) 'Artist statement', https://thedirtycanteen.wordpress.com/ehren-tool/

Vale, Lawrence (2014) *Architecture, Power and National Identity*, New York and London: Routledge.

Vincentelli, Moira (2017) 'Gender, identity and studio ceramics', pp. 342–362 in Andrew Livingstone and Kevin Petrie (eds) (2017) *The Ceramics Reader*, London and New York: Bloomsbury Academic.

de Waal, Edmund (2015) *The White Road: A Journey into Obsession*, London: Vintage.

Walker, Kristen (2008) 'Chilean women's resistance in the arpillera movement', *CETRI*, 30 October 2008, http://www.cetri.be/spip.php?article911&lang=fr

Walker, Melissa, Bronwyn Fredericks, Kyly Mills and Debra Anderson (2014) '"Yarning" as a method for community-based health research with Indigenous women: The Indigenous Women's Wellness Research Program', *Health Care for Women International*, 35(10): 1216–1226.

Wallace, Jacqueline (2012) 'Yarn bombing, knit graffiti and underground brigades: A study of craftivism and mobility', *Journal of Mobile Media*, 6(3), http://wi.mobilities.ca/yarn-bombing-knit-graffiti-and-underground-brigades-a-study-of-craftivism-and-mobility/

84   Bibliography

Walt, Stephen M. (2005) 'The relationship between theory and policy in International Relations', *Annual Review of Political Science*, 8: 23–48.

Walters, Ian (1997) 'Vietnam Zippos', *Journal of Material Culture*, 2(1): 61–75.

Webb, Penny (2015) 'Susan Cohn review: Jewels for life, and death', *The Sydney Morning Herald*, 17 September 2015, https://www.smh.com.au/entertainment/art-and-design/susan-cohn-review-jewels-for-life-and-death-20150917-gjona1.html

Weber, Cynthia (2005 [2001]) *International Relations Theory: A Critical Introduction*, 2nd edition, Oxon and New York: Routledge.

Wedderburn, Alister (2019) 'The appropriation of an icon: *Guernica*, remade', *International Feminist Journal of Politics*, 21(3): 480–487.

Weldes, Jutta (ed.) (2003) *To Seek Out New Worlds*, New York: Palgrave Macmillan.

Weldes, Jutta (2006) 'High politics and low data: Globalization discourses and popular culture', pp. 176–186 in Dvora Yanow and Peregrine Schwartz-Shea (eds) *Interpretation and Method: Empirical Research Methods and the Interpretive Turn*, Armonk, NY: M.E. Sharpe.

Weldes, Jutta and Christina Rowley (2015) 'So, how does popular culture relate to world politics?', pp. 23–34 in Federica Caso and Caitlin Hamilton (eds) *Popular Culture and World Politics: Theories, Methods, Pedagogies*, Bristol: E-IR Publishing.

Westfall, Carol D. (2012) 'Textiles and politics – dishtowels and diatribes', Textile Society of America Symposium Proceedings, paper 757, http://digitalcommons.unl.edu/cgi/viewcontent.cgi?article=1756&context=tsaconf

Wexler Gallery (n.d.) 'Roberto Lugo', https://www.wexlergallery.com/roberto-lugo/

Wheeler, Eileen (2012) 'The political stitch: Voicing resistance in a suffrage textile', Textile Society of America Symposium Proceedings, paper 758, http://digitalcommons.unl.edu/cgi/viewcontent.cgi?article=1757&context=tsaconf

Wibben, Annick T. R. (2011) *Feminist Security Studies: A Narrative Approach*, London and New York: Routledge.

The William Benton Museum of Art (n.d.) 'What is an arpillera?', https://benton.uconn.edu/web-exhibitions-2/arpillera/what-is-an-arpillera/

Woodward, Ian (2007) *Understanding Material Culture*, London, California, New Delhi and Singapore: SAGE Publications.

Woodward, Sophie (2016) 'Object interviews, material imaginings and "unsettling" methods: Interdisciplinary approaches to understanding materials and material culture', *Qualitative Research*, 16(4): 359–374.

Workman, Derek (2012) 'Would you like some salt and pepper? How about 80,000 shakers' worth?', *Smithsonian Magazine*, 23 January 2012, https://www.smithsonianmag.com/travel/would-you-like-some-salt-and-pepper-how-about-80000-shakers-worth-23901227/

World Peace Tartan (n.d.) *Facebook*, https://www.facebook.com/WorldPeaceTartan

Wright, Terence (2008) *Visual Impact: Culture and the Meaning of Images*, Oxford and New York: Berg.

Zeitlin Cooke, Ariel (2005) 'Common threads: The creation of war textiles around the world', pp. 3–29 in Ariel Zeitlin Cooke and Marsha MacDowell (eds) *Weavings of War: Fabrics of Memory*, USA: Michigan State University Museum.

Index

actants 6n6
arpilleras 18–20
artefacts 6–8, 17–18
artefactuality *see* thinginess
Australian Parliament
  House Embroidery
  29–31, 35n7

Barthes, Roland 12n3
Byrne, Penny *55*, 58–59

Cameron, Melissa 40–42
Carnell, Sophie 46, 47n2
ceramics 48–60
clay 48–50
clothes 34n2
coal 44
Cohn, Su san 42–43
colcha embroidery 25–27
colour 19, 22n7, 26, 31–33

Enloe, Cynthia 2
everyday 2–6, 52–53
everyday artefacts of world
  politics 10–11

fabric 20

The Great Tapestry of Scotland
  29–31, 35n7

Hashimoto, Kyoko 43–44
Hmong people 27
Hunt, Barb 32–33

International Relations 2,
  4–5, 13n10

jewellery 36–47
Jørgensen, Marianne 31–33

The Keiskamma Tapestry 29–31,
  30, 35n7
knitting 32–33
The Koh-i-Noor 38
Kouloubi, Erato 44–46, *45*

Lefebvre, Henri 12n1
Ling, L.H.M. 9
Lugo, Roberto 52–53

makers *see* making
making 61–63
Mathieu, Paul 53–55, *54*
Meli Walker, Nancy 39–42

narratives *see* storytelling

Ostrom, Walter 53

Perec, Georges 2–4, 47n2
Pfeiffer, Joel 57–58
pha pra vet 27–29

Rose, Jaine 32–33

Saracino, Stephen F. 40–42
Schobinger, Bernhard 41–42
storytelling 15–18, 21n4, 38

86   *Index*

stuff 7, 63
Sylvester, Christine 5

tartan 24
textiles 24–35, 34n1

thinginess 17, 22n7, 43
Tool, Ehren 56–57
Trujillo, Tiva 27

world politics 8–10